KB186451

한국의 토익 수험자 여러분께,

토익 시험은 세계적인 직무 영어능력 평가 시험으로, 지난 40여 년간 비즈니스 현장에서 필요한 영어능력 평가의 기준을 제시해 왔습니다. 토익 시험 및 토익스피킹, 토익라이팅 시험은 세계에서 가장 널리 통용되는 영어능력 검증 시험으로, 160여 개국 14,000여 기관이 토익 성적을 의사결정에 활용하고 있습니다.

YBM은 한국의 토익 시험을 주관하는 ETS 독점 계약사입니다.

ETS는 한국 수험자들의 효과적인 토익 학습을 돕고자 YBM을 통하여 'ETS 토익 공식 교재'를 독점 출간하고 있습니다. 또한 'ETS 토익 공식 교재' 시리즈에 기출문항을 제공해 한국의 다른 교재들에 수록된 기출을 복제하거나 변형한 문항으로 인하여 발생할 수 있는 수험자들의 혼동을 방지하고 있습니다.

복제 및 변형 문항들은 토익 시험의 출제의도를 벗어날 수 있기 때문에 기출문항을 수록한 'ETS 토익 공식 교재'만큼 시험에 잘 대비할 수 없습니다.

'ETS 토익 공식 교재'를 통하여 수험자 여러분의 영어 소통을 위한 노력에 큰 성취가 있기를 바랍니다.

감사합니다.

Dear TOEIC Test Takers in Korea,

The TOEIC program is the global leader in English-language assessment for the workplace. It has set the standard for assessing English-language skills needed in the workplace for more than 40 years. The TOEIC tests are the most widely used English language assessments around the world, with 14,000+ organizations across more than 160 countries trusting TOEIC scores to make decisions.

YBM is the ETS Country Master Distributor for the TOEIC program in Korea and so is the exclusive distributor for TOEIC Korea.

To support effective learning for TOEIC test-takers in Korea, ETS has authorized YBM to publish the only Official TOEIC prep books in Korea. These books contain actual TOEIC items to help prevent confusion among Korean test-takers that might be caused by other prep book publishers' use of reproduced or paraphrased items.

Reproduced or paraphrased items may fail to reflect the intent of actual TOEIC items and so will not prepare test-takers as well as the actual items contained in the ETS TOEIC Official prep books published by YBM.

We hope that these ETS TOEIC Official prep books enable you, as test-takers, to achieve great success in your efforts to communicate effectively in English.

Thank you.

입문부터 실전까지 수준별 학습을 통해 최단기 목표점수 달성!

ETS TOEIC® 공식수험서
스마트 학습 지원

www.ybmbooks.com에서도 무료 MP3를 다운로드 받을 수 있습니다.

ETS 토익 모바일 학습 플랫폼!
ETS 토익기출 수험서 어플

구글플레이   앱스토어

교재 학습 지원
- 교재 해설 강의
- LC 음원 MP3
- 교재/부록 모의고사 채점 분석
- 단어 암기장

부가 서비스
- 데일리 학습(토익 기출문제 풀이)
- 토익 최신 경향 무료 특강
- 토익 타이머

모의고사 결과 분석
- 파트별/문항별 정답률
- 파트별/유형별 취약점 리포트
- 전체 응시자 점수 분포도

ETS 토익 학습 전용 온라인 커뮤니티!
ETS TOEIC® Book 공식카페

etstoeicbook.co.kr

강사진의 학습 지원   토익 대표강사들의 학습 지원과 멘토링

교재 학습관 운영   교재별 학습게시판을 통해 무료 동영상
강의 등 학습 지원

학습 콘텐츠 제공   토익 학습 콘텐츠와 정기시험
예비특강 업데이트

*toeic®

토익® 정기시험
기출문제집 1
1000
LISTENING

토익 정기시험
기출문제집 1
1000
LISTENING

발행인	허문호
발행처	YBM

편집	노경미, 허유정
디자인	김혜경, 이현숙
마케팅	정연철, 박천산, 고영노, 박찬경, 김동진, 김윤하

초판발행	2018년 12월 17일
35쇄발행	2024년 9월 20일

신고일자	1964년 3월 28일
신고번호	제 1964-000003호
주소	서울시 종로구 종로 104
전화	(02) 2000-0515 [구입문의] / (02) 2000-0429 [내용문의]
팩스	(02) 2285-1523
홈페이지	www.ybmbooks.com

ISBN	978-89-17-23055-0

ETS, TOEIC and 토익 are registered trademarks of Educational Testing Service, Princeton, New Jersey, U.S.A., used in the Republic of Korea under license. Copyright © 2018 by Educational Testing Service, Princeton, New Jersey, U.S.A. All rights reserved. Reproduced under license for limited use by YBM. These materials are protected by United States Laws, International Copyright Laws and International Treaties.
In the event of any discrepancy between this translation and official ETS materials, the terms of the official ETS materials will prevail. All items were created or reviewed by ETS. All item annotations and test-taking tips were reviewed by ETS.

서면에 의한 저자와 출판사의 허락 없이 내용의 일부 혹은 전부를 인용 및 복제하거나 발췌하는 것을 금합니다.
낙장 및 파본은 교환해 드립니다.
구입철회는 구매처 규정에 따라 교환 및 환불처리 됩니다.

✳toeic.

토익® 정기시험 기출문제집 1

1000

LISTENING

Preface

Dear test taker,

English-language proficiency has become a vital tool for success. It can help you excel in business, travel the world, and communicate effectively with friends and colleagues. The TOEIC® test measures your ability to function effectively in English in these types of situations. Because TOEIC scores are recognized around the world as evidence of your English-language proficiency, you will be able to confidently demonstrate your English skills to employers and begin your journey to success.

The test developers at ETS are excited to help you achieve your personal and professional goals through the use of the TOEIC® 정기시험 기출문제집 1000 Vol.1. This book contains test questions taken from actual, official TOEIC tests. It also contains three tests that were developed by ETS to help prepare you for actual TOEIC tests. All these materials will help you become familiar with the TOEIC test's format and content. This book also contains detailed explanations of the question types and language points contained in the TOEIC test. These test questions and explanations have all been prepared by the same test specialists who develop the actual TOEIC test, so you can be confident that you will receive an authentic test-preparation experience.

Features of the TOEIC® 정기시험 기출문제집 1000 Vol.1 include the following.

- Seven full-length actual tests plus three full-length tests of equal quality created by ETS for test preparation use, all accompanied by answer keys and official scripts
- Specific and easy to understand explanations for learners
- The very same ETS voice actors that you will hear in an official TOEIC test administration

---

By using the TOEIC® 정기시험 기출문제집 1000 Vol.1 to prepare for the TOEIC test, you can be assured that you have a professionally prepared resource that will provide you with accurate guidance so that you are more familiar with the tasks, content, and format of the test and that will help you maximize your TOEIC test score. With your official TOEIC score certificate, you will be ready to show the world what you know!

We are delighted to assist you on your TOEIC journey with the TOEIC® 정기시험 기출문제집 1000 Vol.1 and wish you the best of success.

최신 기출문제 전격 공개!

유일무이

'출제기관이 독점 제공한' 기출문제가 담긴 유일한 교재!

이 책에는 정기시험 기출문제 7세트와 토익 예상문제 3세트가 수록되어 있다. 시험에 나온 토익 문제로
실전 감각을 키우고, 동일한 난이도의 예상문제로 시험에 확실하게 대비하자!

국내최고

'정기시험 성우 음성'으로 실전 대비!

이 책에 수록된 10세트의 LC 음원은 모두 실제 시험에서 나온 정기 시험 성우의 음원이다.
시험장에서 듣게 될 음성으로 공부하면 까다로운 영국·호주식 발음도 걱정 없다.

독점제공

'ETS가 제공하는' 표준점수 환산표!

출제기관 ETS가 독점 제공하는 표준점수 환산표를 수록했다. 채점 후 환산표를 통해
자신의 실력이 어느 정도인지 가늠해 보자!

What is the TOEIC?

TOEIC은 어떤 시험인가요?

Test of English for International Communication(국제적 의사소통을 위한 영어 시험)의 약자로서, 영어가 모국어가 아닌 사람들이 일상생활 또는 비즈니스 현장에서 꼭 필요한 실용적 영어 구사 능력을 갖추었는가를 평가하는 시험이다.

시험 구성

구성	Part		내용	문항수	시간	배점
듣기(L/C)	1		사진 묘사	6	45분	495점
	2		질의 & 응답	25		
	3		짧은 대화	39		
	4		짧은 담화	30		
읽기(R/C)	5		단문 빈칸 채우기(문법/어휘)	30	75분	495점
	6		장문 빈칸 채우기	16		
	7	독해	단일 지문	29		
			이중 지문	10		
			삼중 지문	15		
Total	**7 Parts**			**200문항**	**120분**	**990점**

TOEIC 접수는 어떻게 하나요?

TOEIC 접수는 한국 토익 위원회 사이트(www.toeic.co.kr)에서 온라인 상으로만 접수가 가능하다. 사이트에서 매월 자세한 접수 일정과 시험 일정 등의 구체적 정보 확인이 가능하니, 미리 일정을 확인하여 접수하도록 한다.

시험장에 반드시
가져가야 할 준비물은요?

신분증 규정 신분증만 가능

(주민등록증, 운전면허증, 기간 만료 전의 여권, 공무원증 등)

필기구 연필, 지우개 (볼펜이나 사인펜은 사용 금지)

시험은 어떻게
진행되나요?

09:20	입실 (09:50 이후는 입실 불가)
09:30 – 09:45	답안지 작성에 관한 오리엔테이션
09:45 – 09:50	휴식
09:50 – 10:05	신분증 확인
10:05 – 10:10	문제지 배부 및 파본 확인
10:10 – 10:55	듣기 평가 (Listening Test)
10:55 – 12:10	독해 평가 (Reading Test)

TOEIC 성적 확인은
어떻게 하죠?

시험일로부터 약 12일 후, 오후 3시부터 인터넷과 ARS(060-800-0515)로 성적을 확인할 수 있다. TOEIC 성적표는 우편이나 온라인으로 발급 받을 수 있다(시험 접수시, 양자 택일). 우편으로 발급 받을 경우는 성적 발표 후 대략 일주일이 소요되며, 온라인 발급을 선택하면 유효기간 내에 홈페이지에서 본인이 직접 1회에 한해 무료 출력할 수 있다. TOEIC 성적은 시험일로부터 2년간 유효하다.

TOEIC은
몇 점 만점인가요?

TOEIC 점수는 듣기 영역(LC) 점수, 읽기 영역(RC) 점수, 그리고 이 두 영역을 합계한 전체 점수 세 부분으로 구성된다. 각 부분의 점수는 5점 단위이며, 5점에서 495점에 걸쳐 주어지고, 전체 점수는 10점에서 990점까지이며, 만점은 990점이다. TOEIC 성적은 각 문제 유형의 난이도에 따른 점수 환산표에 의해 결정된다.

토익 경향 분석

1인 등장 사진
주어는 He/She, A man/woman, One of the men/women
등이며 주로 앞부분에 나온다.

2인 이상 등장 사진
주어는 They, Some men/women/people 등이며 주로 중간
부분에 나온다.

사물/배경 사진
주어는 A car, Some chairs 등이며 주로 뒷부분에 나온다.

사람 또는 사물 중심 사진
주어가 일부는 사람, 일부는 사물이며 주로 뒷부분에 나온다.

사람 또는
사물 중심 사진
33%

1인
등장 사진
33%

**PART 1
최신 출제 경향**

사물/
배경 사진
17%

2인 이상
등장 사진
17%

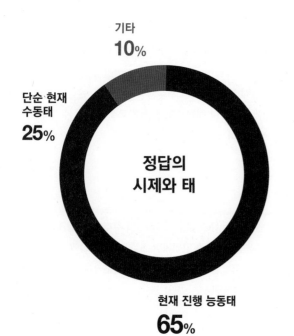

기타
10%

단순 현재
수동태
25%

**정답의
시제와 태**

현재 진행 능동태
65%

현재 진행 능동태
〈is/are + 현재분사〉 형태이며 주로 사람이 주어이다.

단순 현재 수동태
〈is/are + 과거분사〉 형태이며 주로 사물이 주어이다.

기타
〈is/are + being + 과거분사〉 형태의 현재 진행 수동태, 〈has/
have + been + 과거 분사〉 형태의 현재 완료 수동태, '타동사 +
목적어' 형태의 단순 현재 능동태, There is/are와 같은 단순 현
재도 나온다.

평서문
질문이 아니라 객관적인 사실이나 화자의 의견
등을 나타내는 문장이다.

명령문
동사원형이나 Please 등으로 시작한다.

의문사 의문문
각 의문사마다 1~2개씩 나온다. 의문사가 단
독으로 나오기도 하지만 What time ~?, How
long ~?, Which room ~? 등에서처럼 다른 명
사나 형용사와 같이 나오기도 한다.

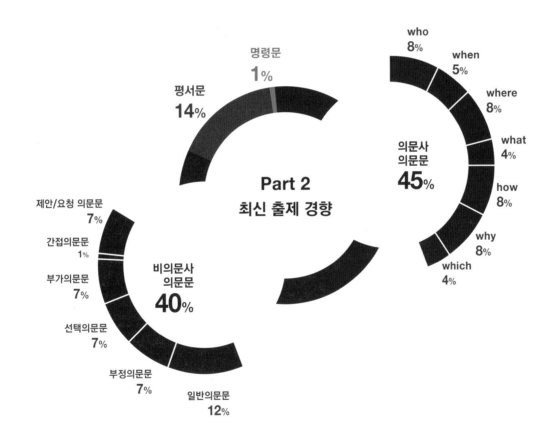

비의문사 의문문
일반(Yes/No) 의문문 적게 나올 때는 한두 개, 많이 나올 때는 서너 개씩 나오는 편이다.
부정의문문 Don't you ~?, Isn't he ~? 등으로 시작하는 문장이며 일반 긍정 의문문보다는 약간 더 적게 나온다.
선택의문문 A or B 형태로 나오며 A와 B의 형태가 단어, 구, 절일 수 있다. 구나 절일 경우 문장이 길어져서 어려워진다.
부가의문문 ~ don't you?, ~ isn't he? 등으로 끝나는 문장이며, 일반 부정 의문문과 비슷하다고 볼 수 있다.
간섭의분분 의문사가 분상 저금 부분이 아니라 문장 중간에 들어 있다.
제안/요청 의문문 정보를 얻기보다는 상대방의 도움이나 동의 등을 얻기 위한 목적이 일반적이다.

PART 3 | 짧은 대화 Short Conversations

- 3인 대화의 경우 남자 화자 두 명과 여자 화자 한 명 또는 남자 화자 한 명과 여자 화자 두 명이 나온다. 따라서 문제에서는 2인 대화에서와 달리 the man이나 the woman이 아니라 the men이나 the women 또는 특정한 이름이 언급될 수 있다.

- 대화 & 시각 정보는 항상 파트의 뒷부분에 나온다.

- 시각 정보의 유형으로 chart, map, floor plan, schedule, table, weather forecast, directory, list, invoice, receipt, sign, packing slip 등 다양한 자료가 골고루 나온다.

2인 대화 & 시각 정보 **23%**
2인 대화 **63%**
3인 대화 **14%**

PART 3 대화의 유형

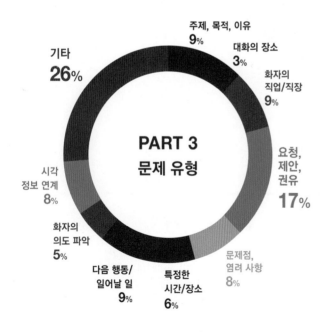

기타 **26%**
주제, 목적, 이유 **9%**
대화의 장소 **3%**
화자의 직업/직장 **9%**
요청, 제안, 권유 **17%**
문제점, 염려 사항 **8%**
특정한 시간/장소 **6%**
다음 행동/일어날 일 **9%**
화자의 의도 파악 **5%**
시각 정보 연계 **8%**

PART 3 문제 유형

- 주제, 목적, 이유, 대화의 장소, 화자의 직업/직장 등과 관련된 문제는 주로 대화의 첫 번째 문제로 나오며 다음 행동/일어날 일 등과 관련된 문제는 주로 대화의 세 번째 문제로 나온다.

- 화자의 의도 파악 문제는 주로 2인 대화에 나오지만, 가끔 3인 대화에 나오기도 한다. 시각 정보 연계 대화에는 나오지 않고 있다.

- Part 3 안에서 화자의 의도 파악 문제는 2개가 나오고 시각 정보 연계 문제는 3개가 나온다.

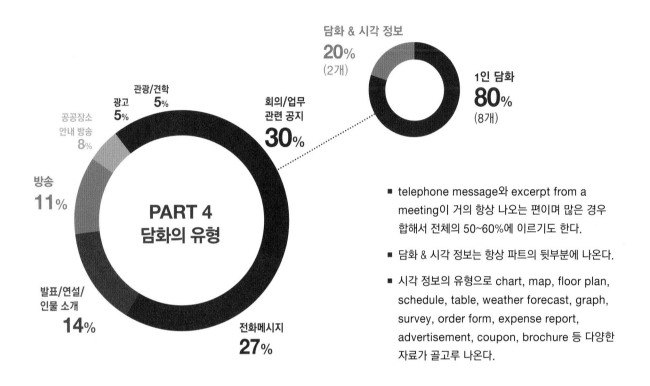

- telephone message와 excerpt from a meeting이 거의 항상 나오는 편이며 많은 경우 합해서 전체의 50~60%에 이르기도 한다.

- 담화 & 시각 정보는 항상 파트의 뒷부분에 나온다.

- 시각 정보의 유형으로 chart, map, floor plan, schedule, table, weather forecast, graph, survey, order form, expense report, advertisement, coupon, brochure 등 다양한 자료가 골고루 나온다.

- 문제 유형은 기본적으로 Part 3과 거의 비슷하다.

- 주제, 목적, 이유, 담화의 장소, 화자의 직업/직장 등과 관련된 문제는 주로 담화의 첫 번째 문제로 나오며 다음 행동/일어날 일 등과 관련된 문제는 주로 담화의 세 번째 문제로 나온다.

- Part 4 안에서 화자의 의도 파악 문제는 3개가 나오고 시각 정보 연계 문제는 2개가 나온다.

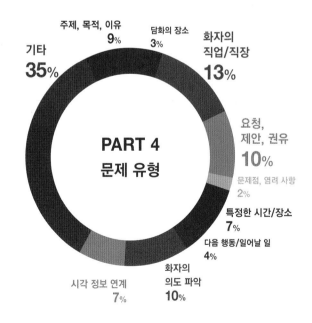

| **PART 5** | 단문 빈칸 채우기 Incomplete Sentences | 총 30문제 |

문법 문제

시제와 대명사와 관련된 문법 문제가 2개씩, 한정사와 분사와 관련된 문법 문제가 1개씩 나온다. 시제 문제의 경우 능동태/수동태나 수의 일치와 연계되기도 한다. 그 밖에 한정사, 능동태/수동태, 부정사, 동명사 등과 관련된 문법 문제가 나온다.

어휘 문제

동사, 명사, 형용사, 부사와 관련된 어휘 문제가 각각 2~3개씩 골고루 나온다. 전치사 어휘 문제는 3개씩 꾸준히 나오지만, 접속사나 어구와 관련된 어휘 문제는 나오지 않을 때도 있고 3개가 나올 때도 있다.

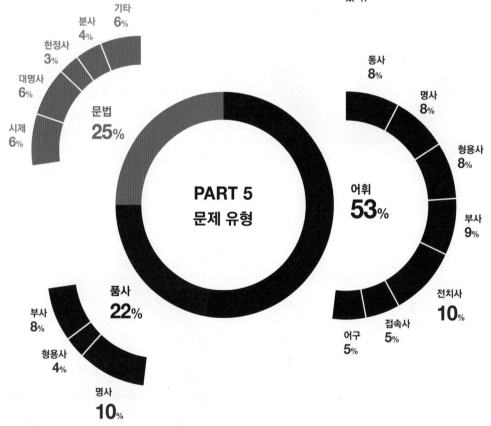

품사 문제

명사와 부사와 관련된 품사 문제가 2~3개씩 나오며, 형용사와 관련된 품사 문제가 상대적으로 적은 편이다.

한 지문에 4문제가 나오며 평균적으로 어휘 문제가 2개, 품사나
문법 문제가 1개, 문맥에 맞는 문장 고르기 문제가 1개 들어간다.
문맥에 맞는 문장 고르기 문제를 제외하면 문제 유형은 기본적
으로 파트 5와 거의 비슷하다.

어휘 문제

동사, 명사, 부사, 어구와 관련된 어휘 문제는 매번
1~2개씩 나온다. 부사 어휘 문제의 경우 therefore(그
러므로)나 however(하지만)처럼 문맥의 흐름을 자연
스럽게 연결해 주는 부사가 자주 나온다.

문맥에 맞는 문장 고르기

문맥에 맞는 문장 고르기 문제는 지문당 한 문제씩
나오는데, 나오는 위치의 확률은 4문제 중 두 번째
문제, 세 번째 문제, 네 번째 문제, 첫 번째 문제
순으로 높다.

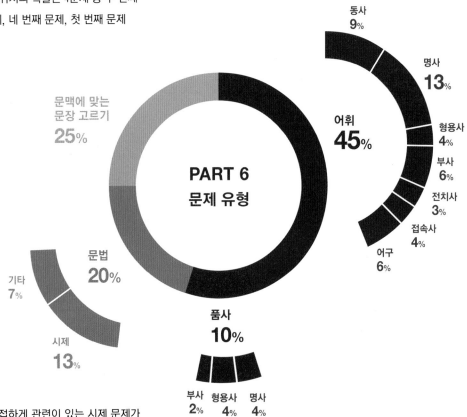

문법 문제

문맥의 흐름과 밀접하게 관련이 있는 시제 문제가
2개 정도 나오며, 능동태/수동태나 수의 일치와
연계되기도 한다. 그 밖에 대명사, 능동태/수동태,
부정사, 접속사/전치사 등과 관련된 문법 문제가
나온다.

품사 문제

명사나 형용사 문제가 부사 문제보다 좀 더
지주 나온다.

| PART 7 | 독해 Reading Comprehension |

지문 유형	지문당 문제 수	지문 개수	비중 %
단일 지문	2문항	4개	약 15%
	3문항	3개	약 16%
	4문항	3개	약 22%
이중 지문	5문항	2개	약 19%
삼중 지문	5문항	3개	약 28%

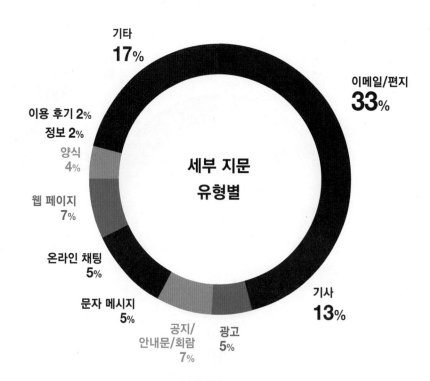

■ 이메일/편지, 기사 유형 지문은 거의 항상 나오는 편이며 많은 경우 합해서 전체의 50~60%에 이르기도 한다.

■ 기타 지문 유형으로 agenda, brochure, comment card, coupon, flyer, instructions, invitation, invoice, list, menu, page from a catalog, policy statement, report, schedule, survey, voucher 등 다양한 자료가 골고루 나온다.

(이중 지문과 삼중 지문 속의 지문들을 모두 낱개로 계산함 – 총 23지문)

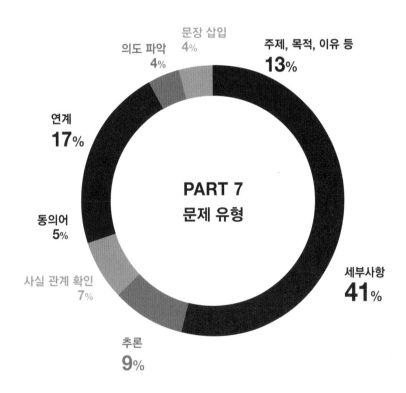

- 동의어 문제는 주로 이중 지문이나 삼중 지문에 나온다.
- 연계 문제는 일반적으로 이중 지문에서 한 문제, 삼중 지문에서 두 문제가 나온다.
- 의도 파악 문제는 문자 메시지(text-message chain)나 온라인 채팅(online chat discussion) 지문에서 출제되며 두 문제가
  나온다.
- 문장 삽입 문제는 주로 기사, 이메일, 편지, 회람 지문에서 줄제되며 두 분제가 나온나.

점수 환산표 및 산출법

점수 환산표 이 책에 수록된 각 Test를 풀고 난 후, 맞은 개수를 세어 점수를 환산해 보세요.

LISTENING Raw Score (맞은 개수)	LISTENING Scaled Score (환산 점수)	READING Raw Score (맞은 개수)	READING Scaled Score (환산 점수)
96–100	475–495	96–100	460–495
91–95	435–495	91–95	425–490
86–90	405–475	86–90	395–465
81–85	370–450	81–85	370–440
76–80	345–420	76–80	335–415
71–75	320–390	71–75	310–390
66–70	290–360	66–70	280–365
61–65	265–335	61–65	250–335
56–60	235–310	56–60	220–305
51–55	210–280	51–55	195–270
46–50	180–255	46–50	165–240
41–45	155–230	41–45	140–215
36–40	125–205	36–40	115–180
31–35	105–175	31–35	95–145
26–30	85–145	26–30	75–120
21–25	60–115	21–25	60–95
16–20	30–90	16–20	45–75
11–15	5–70	11–15	30–55
6–10	5–60	6–10	10–40
1–5	5–50	1–5	5–30
0	5–35	0	5–15

점수 산출 방법   아래의 방식으로 점수를 산출할 수 있다.

STEP 1

자신의 답안을 수록된 정답과 대조하여 채점한다. 각 Section의 맞은 개수가 본인의 Section별 '실제 점수 (통계 처리하기 전의 점수, raw score)'이다. Listening Test와 Reading Test의 정답 수를 세어, 자신의 실제 점수를 아래의 해당란에 기록한다.

	맞은 개수	환산 점수대
LISTENING		
READING		
총점		

Section별 실제 점수가 그대로 Section별 TOEIC 점수가 되는 것은 아니다. TOEIC은 시행할 때마다 별도로 특정한 통계 처리 방법을 사용하며 이러한 실제 점수를 환산 점수(converted[scaled] score) 로 전환하게 된다. 이렇게 전환함으로써, 매번 시행될 때마다 문제는 달라지지만 그 점수가 갖는 의미는 같아지게 된다. 예를 들어 어느 한 시험에서 총점 550점의 성적으로 받는 실력이라면 다른 시험에서도 거의 550점대의 성적을 받게 되는 것이다.

▼

STEP 2

실제 점수를 위 표에 기록한 후 왼쪽 페이지의 점수 환산표를 보도록 한다. TOEIC이 시행될 때마다 대 개 이와 비슷한 형태의 표가 작성되는데, 여기 제시된 환산표는 본 교재에 수록된 Test용으로 개발된 것이다. 이 표를 사용하여 자신의 실제 점수를 환산 점수로 전환하도록 한다. 즉, 예를 들어 Listening Test의 실제 정답 수가 61~65개이면 환산 점수는 265점에서 335점 사이가 된다. 여기서 실제 정답 수 가 61개이면 환산 점수가 265점이고, 65개이면 환산 점수가 335점 임을 의미하는 것은 아니다. 본 책 의 Test를 위해 작성된 이 점수 환산표가 자신의 영어 실력이 어느 정도인지 대략적으로 파악하는 데 도 움이 되긴 하지만, 이 표가 실제 TOEIC 성적 산출에 그대로 사용된 적은 없다는 사실을 밝혀 둔다.

토익® 정기시험
기출문제집

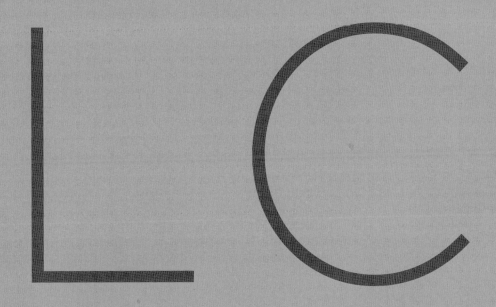

LC

기출 TEST

01

LISTENING TEST

In the Listening test, you will be asked to demonstrate how well you understand spoken English. The entire Listening test will last approximately 45 minutes. There are four parts, and directions are given for each part. You must mark your answers on the separate answer sheet. Do not write your answers in your test book.

PART 1

Directions: For each question in this part, you will hear four statements about a picture in your test book. When you hear the statements, you must select the one statement that best describes what you see in the picture. Then find the number of the question on your answer sheet and mark your answer. The statements will not be printed in your test book and will be spoken only one time.

Statement (C), "They're sitting at a table," is the best description of the picture, so you should select answer (C) and mark it on your answer sheet.

1.

2.

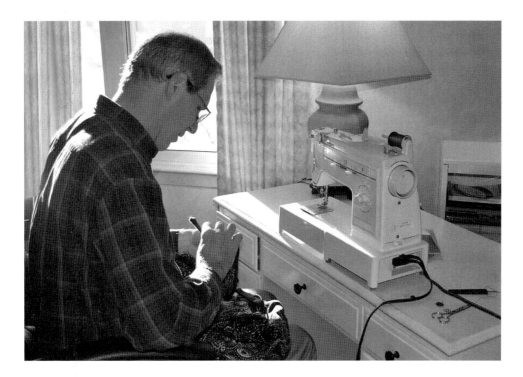

GO ON TO THE NEXT PAGE

3.

4.

5.

6.

GO ON TO THE NEXT PAGE ➤

PART 2

Directions: You will hear a question or statement and three responses spoken in English. They will not be printed in your test book and will be spoken only one time. Select the best response to the question or statement and mark the letter (A), (B), or (C) on your answer sheet.

7. Mark your answer on your answer sheet.

8. Mark your answer on your answer sheet.

9. Mark your answer on your answer sheet.

10. Mark your answer on your answer sheet.

11. Mark your answer on your answer sheet.

12. Mark your answer on your answer sheet.

13. Mark your answer on your answer sheet.

14. Mark your answer on your answer sheet.

15. Mark your answer on your answer sheet.

16. Mark your answer on your answer sheet.

17. Mark your answer on your answer sheet.

18. Mark your answer on your answer sheet.

19. Mark your answer on your answer sheet.

20. Mark your answer on your answer sheet.

21. Mark your answer on your answer sheet.

22. Mark your answer on your answer sheet.

23. Mark your answer on your answer sheet.

24. Mark your answer on your answer sheet.

25. Mark your answer on your answer sheet.

26. Mark your answer on your answer sheet.

27. Mark your answer on your answer sheet.

28. Mark your answer on your answer sheet.

29. Mark your answer on your answer sheet.

30. Mark your answer on your answer sheet.

31. Mark your answer on your answer sheet.

PART 3

Directions: You will hear some conversations between two or more people. You will be asked to answer three questions about what the speakers say in each conversation. Select the best response to each question and mark the letter (A), (B), (C), or (D) on your answer sheet. The conversations will not be printed in your test book and will be spoken only one time.

32. Why is the woman calling?
    (A) To make an appointment
    (B) To rent a car
    (C) To ask about a fee
    (D) To apply for a position

33. According to the man, what has recently changed?
    (A) Office hours
    (B) Job requirements
    (C) A computer system
    (D) A company policy

34. What does the man agree to do?
    (A) Waive a fee
    (B) Reschedule a meeting
    (C) Sign a contract
    (D) Repair a vehicle

35. What is the topic of the conversation?
    (A) Health
    (B) Traffic
    (C) Sports
    (D) Finance

36. What caused a problem?
    (A) A staffing change
    (B) A rainstorm
    (C) A typographical error
    (D) A road closure

37. What will the listeners hear next?
    (A) A commercial
    (B) A song
    (C) A weather report
    (D) A reading from a book

38. What does the woman notify the man about?
    (A) She is unable to meet a deadline.
    (B) She needs a replacement laptop.
    (C) She cannot attend a business trip.
    (D) She is planning to give a speech.

39. According to the woman, what recently happened in her department?
    (A) A corporate policy was updated.
    (B) A supply order was mishandled.
    (C) Client contracts were renewed.
    (D) New employees were hired.

40. What does the man say he will do next?
    (A) Speak with a colleague
    (B) Conduct an interview
    (C) Calculate a budget
    (D) Draft a travel itinerary

41. What does the man want to do?
    (A) Purchase an area map
    (B) See an event schedule
    (C) Cancel a hotel reservation
    (D) Book a bus tour

42. What is the man asked to choose?
    (A) When to arrive
    (B) What to visit
    (C) How to pay
    (D) What to eat

43. What does the woman suggest doing?
    (A) Wearing a jacket
    (B) Using a credit card
    (C) Bringing a camera
    (D) Looking for a coupon

GO ON TO THE NEXT PAGE

44. What does the man offer to do?

    (A) Meet in the lobby
    (B) Contact a receptionist
    (C) Carry some files
    (D) Delay a meeting

45. According to the man, what happened last week?

    (A) An office door would not lock.
    (B) A sink was installed incorrectly.
    (C) An elevator stopped working.
    (D) A document was lost.

46. Why does the woman say, "a piece of hardware had to be custom made"?

    (A) To justify a price
    (B) To explain a delay
    (C) To illustrate a product's age
    (D) To express regret for a purchase

---

47. What product are the speakers discussing?

    (A) Electronics
    (B) Office furniture
    (C) Calendars
    (D) Clothing

48. What does Donna suggest?

    (A) Hiring additional staff
    (B) Revising a budget
    (C) Posting some photos online
    (D) Reducing prices

49. What does the man propose?

    (A) Postponing a decision
    (B) Conducting a survey
    (C) Developing new products
    (D) Opening another location

---

50. Who most likely is the man?

    (A) A manager
    (B) A consultant
    (C) A client
    (D) A trainee

51. What does the woman ask the man for?

    (A) Some feedback
    (B) Some assistance
    (C) Some references
    (D) Some dates

52. What will the man receive?

    (A) Extra time off
    (B) A promotion
    (C) Bonus pay
    (D) An award

---

53. What type of product is being discussed?

    (A) A musical instrument
    (B) A kitchen appliance
    (C) A power tool
    (D) A tablet computer

54. Which product feature is the man most proud of?

    (A) The battery life
    (B) The color selection
    (C) The sound quality
    (D) The size

55. Why does the man say, "my favorite singer is performing that night"?

    (A) To request a schedule change
    (B) To explain a late arrival
    (C) To decline an invitation
    (D) To recommend a musician

---

56. What type of event is being planned?

(A) A trade show
(B) An awards ceremony
(C) A film festival
(D) A wedding

57. What does the man ask about?

(A) Accommodations
(B) Entertainment
(C) Meal options
(D) Outdoor seating

58. What does the hotel offer for free?

(A) Meals
(B) Internet access
(C) Transportation
(D) Parking

59. What problem does the man mention?

(A) His car is out of fuel.
(B) His phone battery is empty.
(C) He is late for an appointment.
(D) He forgot his wallet.

60. Where are the speakers?

(A) At a train station
(B) At an electronics repair shop
(C) At a furniture store
(D) At a coffee shop

61. What does the woman suggest the man do?

(A) Check a Web site
(B) Call a taxi
(C) Return at a later time
(D) Go to the library

Medical Lab	ID code
Blood test	018
Allergy test	019
Body Fat test	020
X-ray	021

62. What is the man having trouble with?

(A) Conducting a test
(B) Preparing a bill
(C) Contacting a patient
(D) Shipping an order

63. Look at the graphic. Which code should the man use?

(A) 018
(B) 019
(C) 020
(D) 021

64. What does the woman say will happen soon?

(A) Some patients will be transferred to another doctor.
(B) Some employees will join a medical practice.
(C) A list will be available electronically.
(D) A doctor will begin a medical procedure.

GO ON TO THE NEXT PAGE

Logo:	Anvi Designs
Size:	Large
Material:	100% Cotton
Care Instructions:	Wash in Warm Water
Origin:	Made in India

65. What does the woman say they will need to do?

    (A) Rent storage space
    (B) Increase production
    (C) Organize a fashion show
    (D) Update some equipment

66. What does the man suggest?

    (A) Conferring with a client
    (B) Contacting another department
    (C) Photographing some designs
    (D) Changing suppliers

67. Look at the graphic. Which section of the label will the man need to revise?

    (A) The logo
    (B) The material
    (C) The care instructions
    (D) The country of origin

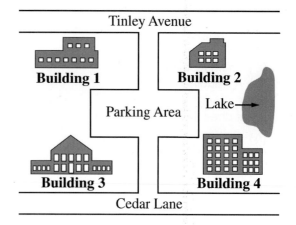

68. What are the speakers mainly discussing?

    (A) A job interview
    (B) A company celebration
    (C) An office relocation
    (D) A landscaping project

69. Look at the graphic. Which building is Silverby Industries located in?

    (A) Building 1
    (B) Building 2
    (C) Building 3
    (D) Building 4

70. What does the woman tell the man about parking?

    (A) He should park in a visitor's space.
    (B) He will have to pay at a meter.
    (C) A parking pass is required.
    (D) The parking area fills up quickly.

PART 4

Directions: You will hear some talks given by a single speaker. You will be asked to answer three questions about what the speaker says in each talk. Select the best response to each question and mark the letter (A), (B), (C), or (D) on your answer sheet. The talks will not be printed in your test book and will be spoken only one time.

71. What type of business is being advertised?

(A) A farmers market
(B) A fitness center
(C) A medical clinic
(D) A sporting goods store

72. What will the listeners be able to do starting in April?

(A) Use multiple locations
(B) Try free samples
(C) Meet with a nutritionist
(D) Enter a contest

73. Why does the speaker invite the listeners to visit a Web site?

(A) To write a review
(B) To register for a class
(C) To check a policy
(D) To look at a map

74. Why does the speaker thank the listeners?

(A) For submitting design ideas
(B) For training new employees
(C) For working overtime
(D) For earning a certification

75. According to the speaker, what is scheduled for next month?

(A) A retirement celebration
(B) A trade show
(C) A factory tour
(D) A store opening

76. What does the speaker imply when she says, "it's a large space"?

(A) There is room to display new merchandise.
(B) High attendance is anticipated.
(C) A venue is too expensive.
(D) There is not enough staff for an event.

77. According to the speaker, what is special about the restaurant?

(A) It has private outdoor seating.
(B) It has been recently renovated.
(C) It has a vegetable garden.
(D) It has weekly cooking classes.

78. Who is Natasha?

(A) A business owner
(B) An interior decorator
(C) An event organizer
(D) A food writer

79. Why does the speaker say, "I eat it all the time"?

(A) He wants to eat something different.
(B) He is recommending a dish.
(C) He knows the ingredients.
(D) He understands a dish is popular.

80. Where is the announcement being made?

(A) On a bus
(B) On a ferry boat
(C) On a train
(D) On an airplane

81. What problem does the speaker mention?

(A) There is no more room for large bags.
(B) Too many tickets have been sold.
(C) Weather conditions have changed.
(D) A piece of equipment is being repaired.

82. According to the speaker, why should the listeners talk with a staff member?

(A) To receive a voucher
(B) To reserve a seat
(C) To buy some food
(D) To get free headphones

GO ON TO THE NEXT PAGE

83. Who is the speaker?

  (A) A repair person
  (B) A store clerk
  (C) A factory worker
  (D) A truck driver

84. What does the company sell?

  (A) Household furniture
  (B) Kitchen appliances
  (C) Packaged foods
  (D) Construction equipment

85. What does the speaker imply when she says, "all I see are houses"?

  (A) She is concerned about some regulations.
  (B) She thinks a mistake has been made.
  (C) A loan application has been completed.
  (D) A development plan cannot be approved.

86. What is the talk mainly about?

  (A) A mobile phone model
  (B) An office security system
  (C) High-speed Internet service
  (D) Business scheduling software

87. Why did the company choose the product?

  (A) It makes arranging meetings easy.
  (B) It is reasonably priced.
  (C) It has good security features.
  (D) It has received positive reviews.

88. What does the speaker say is offered with the product?

  (A) An annual upgrade
  (B) A money-back guarantee
  (C) A mobile phone application
  (D) A customer-service help line

89. What does the speaker say has recently been announced?

  (A) An increase in funding
  (B) A factory opening
  (C) A new venue for an event
  (D) A change in regulations

90. According to the speaker, why do some people dislike a construction project?

  (A) Because it caused a power outage
  (B) Because it costs too much
  (C) Because roads have been closed
  (D) Because of the loud noise

91. What will the speaker do next?

  (A) Introduce an advertiser
  (B) Attend a press conference
  (C) Interview some people
  (D) End a broadcast

92. What does the speaker thank the listeners for?

  (A) Reorganizing some files
  (B) Cleaning a work area
  (C) Working on a Saturday
  (D) Attending a training

93. In which division do the listeners most likely work?

  (A) Shipping and Receiving
  (B) Maintenance
  (C) Sales and Marketing
  (D) Accounting

94. What does the speaker say he will provide?

  (A) A building name
  (B) Group numbers
  (C) Shift schedules
  (D) A temporary password

Saturday	Sunday	Monday	Tuesday
Partly Sunny	Cloudy	Rain	Rain

95. What event is being described?

(A) A sports competition
(B) A government ceremony
(C) A music festival
(D) A cooking contest

96. According to the speaker, what can the listeners find on a Web site?

(A) A city map
(B) A list of vendors
(C) A demonstration video
(D) An entry form

97. Look at the graphic. Which day is the event being held?

(A) Saturday
(B) Sunday
(C) Monday
(D) Tuesday

Westside Technology Conference April 6	
8:00	Protecting Your Data, Carla Wynn
9:00	Learning to Code, Jae-Ho Kim
10:00	Latest Devices, Kaori Aoki
11:00	Is Newer Better?, Alex Lehmann
12:00	Lunch

98. What is the purpose of the call?

(A) To confirm a deadline
(B) To explain a company policy
(C) To make a job offer
(D) To discuss a new product

99. Look at the graphic. Who is the speaker calling?

(A) Carla Wynn
(B) Jae-Ho Kim
(C) Kaori Aoki
(D) Alex Lehmann

100. What does the speaker ask the listener to do?

(A) Check a catalog
(B) Send fee information
(C) Submit a travel itinerary
(D) Update a conference schedule

This is the end of the Listening test.

토익® 정기시험
기출문제집

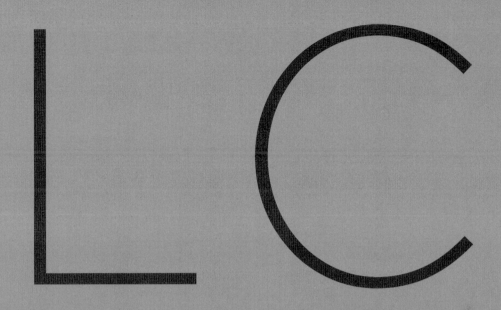

LC

기출 TEST

02

LISTENING TEST

In the Listening test, you will be asked to demonstrate how well you understand spoken English. The entire Listening test will last approximately 45 minutes. There are four parts, and directions are given for each part. You must mark your answers on the separate answer sheet. Do not write your answers in your test book.

PART 1

Directions: For each question in this part, you will hear four statements about a picture in your test book. When you hear the statements, you must select the one statement that best describes what you see in the picture. Then find the number of the question on your answer sheet and mark your answer. The statements will not be printed in your test book and will be spoken only one time.

Statement (C), "They're sitting at a table," is the best description of the picture, so you should select answer (C) and mark it on your answer sheet.

1.

2.

GO ON TO THE NEXT PAGE

3.

4.

5.

6.

GO ON TO THE NEXT PAGE

PART 2

Directions: You will hear a question or statement and three responses spoken in English. They will not be printed in your test book and will be spoken only one time. Select the best response to the question or statement and mark the letter (A), (B), or (C) on your answer sheet.

7. Mark your answer on your answer sheet.

8. Mark your answer on your answer sheet.

9. Mark your answer on your answer sheet.

10. Mark your answer on your answer sheet.

11. Mark your answer on your answer sheet.

12. Mark your answer on your answer sheet.

13. Mark your answer on your answer sheet.

14. Mark your answer on your answer sheet.

15. Mark your answer on your answer sheet.

16. Mark your answer on your answer sheet.

17. Mark your answer on your answer sheet.

18. Mark your answer on your answer sheet.

19. Mark your answer on your answer sheet.

20. Mark your answer on your answer sheet.

21. Mark your answer on your answer sheet.

22. Mark your answer on your answer sheet.

23. Mark your answer on your answer sheet.

24. Mark your answer on your answer sheet.

25. Mark your answer on your answer sheet.

26. Mark your answer on your answer sheet.

27. Mark your answer on your answer sheet.

28. Mark your answer on your answer sheet.

29. Mark your answer on your answer sheet.

30. Mark your answer on your answer sheet.

31. Mark your answer on your answer sheet.

PART 3

Directions: You will hear some conversations between two or more people. You will be asked to answer three questions about what the speakers say in each conversation. Select the best response to each question and mark the letter (A), (B), (C), or (D) on your answer sheet. The conversations will not be printed in your test book and will be spoken only one time.

32. What is the main topic of the conversation?

(A) A new supervisor
(B) A budget report
(C) An office floor plan
(D) A project deadline

33. What does the man request?

(A) Additional office supplies
(B) Extra team members
(C) A different office
(D) A sample document

34. What does the woman suggest the man do?

(A) Speak with a colleague
(B) Organize some files
(C) Revise a manual
(D) E-mail a memo

35. Who most likely is the woman?

(A) A journalist
(B) A musician
(C) A theater director
(D) A costume designer

36. What does the woman ask about?

(A) A performance date
(B) A guest list
(C) Some seating assignments
(D) Some lighting

37. What does the man say he would prefer to do?

(A) Complete a task at a later time
(B) Ask for a meal to be delivered
(C) Speak with a manager
(D) Conduct some background research

38. What is the problem?

(A) There is a scheduling conflict.
(B) There are no projectors available.
(C) A contract is incorrect.
(D) A deadline has been missed.

39. What does the woman inquire about?

(A) Comparing competitors' prices
(B) Purchasing new software
(C) Postponing a training session
(D) Arranging a teleconference

40. What does the man say he will do?

(A) Send some materials
(B) Find some supplies
(C) Speak with a supervisor
(D) Contact a client

41. Where most likely are the speakers?

(A) At a medical office
(B) At a bank
(C) At an electronics store
(D) At a library

42. According to the woman, why should Mr. Patel open an account?

(A) To view a presentation
(B) To make an appointment
(C) To receive a free gift
(D) To leave some feedback

43. What does Colin give to Mr. Patel?

(A) An application
(B) A receipt
(C) A registration card
(D) A set of instructions

GO ON TO THE NEXT PAGE

44. What does the man say will take place in two weeks?

(A) An awards ceremony
(B) A staff retreat
(C) A grand opening celebration
(D) A professional conference

45. What does the woman say she is concerned about?

(A) An inconvenient location
(B) A missed deadline
(C) A parking fee
(D) A canceled flight

46. Why does the man say, "it's twenty dollars to take a taxi"?

(A) To make a suggestion
(B) To express surprise
(C) To complain about a price
(D) To correct a mistake

47. Where do the speakers most likely work?

(A) At a local hotel
(B) At an employment agency
(C) At a clothing manufacturer
(D) At a laundry service

48. What problem does the man mention?

(A) A machine is broken.
(B) A deadline is not realistic.
(C) An item is poorly made.
(D) A supplier went out of business.

49. How will the speakers solve the problem?

(A) By hiring additional staff
(B) By purchasing more material
(C) By updating some machinery
(D) By negotiating with a business

50. What has the woman forgotten to bring?

(A) A receipt for an item
(B) A loyalty card
(C) Some coupons
(D) Some shopping bags

51. What problem does the man mention?

(A) A manager is not available.
(B) A product is out of stock.
(C) A computer system is not working.
(D) An advertised price is incorrect.

52. What does the man imply when he says, "I know where it belongs"?

(A) He can tell the woman where to find an item.
(B) He will return an item to the correct location.
(C) A supervisor is not available.
(D) An item has been put on the wrong shelf.

53. Who most likely is the man?

(A) A professional athlete
(B) A store manager
(C) A city official
(D) A television producer

54. What are the speakers discussing?

(A) A health and fitness show
(B) A workplace volunteer event
(C) A road-repair initiative
(D) A bicycle-sharing program

55. What does the woman say is part of the service her company provides?

(A) Wellness screening
(B) Local advertising
(C) Product samples
(D) Event tickets

56. What is the woman announcing?

(A) A design has been approved.
(B) Some employees will be promoted.
(C) Some equipment will be installed.
(D) A security inspection will take place soon.

57. What is being arranged for next week?

(A) A board meeting
(B) A training session
(C) A company luncheon
(D) A job interview

58. What does the woman say she will do?

(A) Confirm a time
(B) Test some software
(C) Visit a facility
(D) Review a proposal

59. Who most likely is the woman?

(A) A journalist
(B) A mechanic
(C) An engineer
(D) A plant supervisor

60. What is the main topic of the conversation?

(A) New car designs
(B) The opening of a factory
(C) An increase in costs
(D) Safety ratings

61. According to the man, what will happen in December?

(A) Discounted trips will be available.
(B) An advertising campaign will start.
(C) An article will be published.
(D) Production will begin at a facility.

Wood Flooring Options	
Product Code	Type Of Wood
W32	Maple
W51	Oak
W76	Pine
W94	Ash

62. How did the woman reach her decision?

(A) She did some Internet research.
(B) She asked a friend for a recommendation.
(C) She examined some samples.
(D) She compared prices.

63. Look at the graphic. Which product did the woman choose?

(A) W32
(B) W51
(C) W76
(D) W94

64. Why does the man need to call back later?

(A) He is unsure about some inventory.
(B) He is about to attend a meeting.
(C) He needs to check his work schedule.
(D) He wants to consult a coworker.

GO ON TO THE NEXT PAGE

Stockton Community Festival

November 5 and 6
Rain Dates: November 12 and 13

Enjoy local shopping and dining!

Natural History Museum

Mammal Hall	Bird Hall	Main Hall	Cafeteria

65. Who most likely are the speakers?

(A) Community organizers
(B) Weather reporters
(C) Jewelry designers
(D) Restaurant staff

66. Look at the graphic. When will the man work at the festival?

(A) On November 5
(B) On November 6
(C) On November 12
(D) On November 13

67. What does the woman say she will do?

(A) Hang up some posters
(B) Assist a friend
(C) Prepare some food
(D) Write a review

68. Why does the woman talk to the man?

(A) To purchase a ticket
(B) To sign up for a tour
(C) To rent some equipment
(D) To inquire about an exhibit

69. Look at the graphic. Where does the man tell the woman to go?

(A) To the Mammal Hall
(B) To the Bird Hall
(C) To the Main Hall
(D) To the Cafeteria

70. What does the man say about the woman's ticket?

(A) It can be purchased in advance.
(B) It includes admission to special events.
(C) It is issued only to museum members.
(D) It is nonrefundable.

PART 4

Directions: You will hear some talks given by a single speaker. You will be asked to answer three questions about what the speaker says in each talk. Select the best response to each question and mark the letter (A), (B), (C), or (D) on your answer sheet. The talks will not be printed in your test book and will be spoken only one time.

71. Where is the announcement being made?

(A) At an art supply store
(B) At a public library
(C) At a school
(D) At a hardware store

72. What can listeners find on the first floor?

(A) A product demonstration
(B) A discussion-group meeting
(C) Refreshments
(D) Items on sale

73. What are listeners encouraged to do by August 30 ?

(A) Activate a rewards card
(B) Enter a contest
(C) Register for a class
(D) Fill out surveys

74. Who most likely is the speaker?

(A) An appliance salesperson
(B) A repair technician
(C) An apartment manager
(D) A hotel receptionist

75. What is the speaker calling about?

(A) An advertised rebate
(B) An expired warranty
(C) An inaccessible parking space
(D) A broken appliance

76. Why is the listener asked to stop by an office?

(A) To return a key
(B) To collect a package
(C) To drop off a letter
(D) To make a payment

77. What product is the speaker discussing?

(A) A tablet computer
(B) A mobile phone
(C) A radio
(D) A clock

78. What is unique about the product?

(A) Its screen
(B) Its low price
(C) Its range of options
(D) Its size

79. What does the speaker suggest some listeners do?

(A) Call a customer service number
(B) Recycle older products
(C) Visit a sales booth
(D) Log on to a Web site

80. Why has the meeting been called?

(A) To explain a manufacturing process
(B) To announce a merger
(C) To provide details on a contract
(D) To inform employees of an error

81. Why does the speaker say, "It's been a week"?

(A) To express concern about a delay
(B) To praise a team's performance
(C) To remind employees about a rule
(D) To agree with a business strategy

82. What does the speaker ask Masaki to do?

(A) Call a shipping company
(B) Verify some addresses
(C) E-mail staff members
(D) Give a speech

GO ON TO THE NEXT PAGE

83. Which department does the speaker work for?

(A) Building Security
(B) Public Relations
(C) Technology
(D) Payroll

84. What does the speaker ask the listener to do?

(A) Train her on some software
(B) Send an employee to her office
(C) Check some payment information
(D) Attend an orientation

85. What does the speaker mean when she says, "This form is only one page, though"?

(A) A policy has been changed.
(B) A task should not take long.
(C) The wrong document was given out.
(D) Some instructions are unclear.

86. What product will listeners learn about on the tour?

(A) Watches
(B) Computers
(C) Knives
(D) Batteries

87. Who is Laura Shen?

(A) A company president
(B) A news journalist
(C) A scientist
(D) A client

88. What does the speaker mention about the tour?

(A) Large bags are not allowed.
(B) Photography is not permitted.
(C) The size of a group is limited.
(D) Registration is required.

89. Who most likely is the speaker?

(A) A travel agent
(B) A chef
(C) A farmer
(D) A filmmaker

90. What caused a delay?

(A) Equipment problems
(B) Poor weather conditions
(C) Heavy traffic
(D) Lost luggage

91. Why does the speaker say, "I'll be answering questions when it's over"?

(A) To explain that he will be busy
(B) To ask listeners not to interrupt him now
(C) To encourage people to stay afterward
(D) To correct a scheduling mistake

92. Who is the speaker congratulating?

(A) Executive board members
(B) A new business partner
(C) Marketing staff
(D) Food scientists

93. According to the speaker, what do customers like about the commercial?

(A) The images of families
(B) The video quality
(C) The professional actors
(D) The background music

94. What most likely will listeners do next week?

(A) Interview candidates
(B) Share ideas
(C) Check some statistics
(D) Develop a recipe

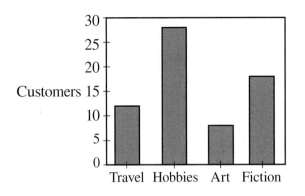

Passenger:
James Albertson

Flight: **Gate:**   **Seat:**
WA15   B12   7A

Boarding Zone: 1

95. What is the announcement about?

(A) Connecting flight information
(B) A lost item
(C) A flight cancellation
(D) A gate change

96. Look at the graphic. Which number should James Albertson pay attention to now?

(A) WA15
(B) B12
(C) 7A
(D) 1

97. What will the speaker announce later?

(A) Where to find luggage
(B) How to select a new seat
(C) Whom to contact for a refund
(D) When repairs will be finished

98. What event did the speaker recently attend?

(A) An advertising seminar
(B) An awards ceremony
(C) A managers' meeting
(D) A writing workshop

99. What topic does the speaker report on?

(A) Company finances
(B) Human resources
(C) Advertising
(D) Competitors

100. Look at the graphic. Which store section will be expanded?

(A) Travel
(B) Hobbies
(C) Art
(D) Fiction

This is the end of the Listening test.

토익® 정기시험
기출문제집

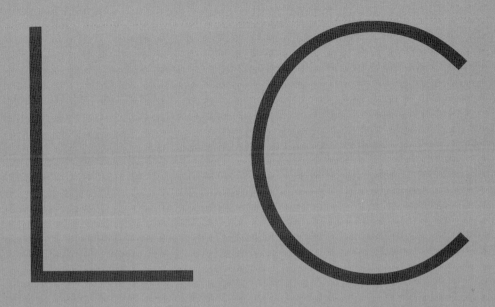

LC

기출 TEST

03

LISTENING TEST

In the Listening test, you will be asked to demonstrate how well you understand spoken English. The entire Listening test will last approximately 45 minutes. There are four parts, and directions are given for each part. You must mark your answers on the separate answer sheet. Do not write your answers in your test book.

PART 1

Directions: For each question in this part, you will hear four statements about a picture in your test book. When you hear the statements, you must select the one statement that best describes what you see in the picture. Then find the number of the question on your answer sheet and mark your answer. The statements will not be printed in your test book and will be spoken only one time.

Statement (C), "They're sitting at a table," is the best description of the picture, so you should select answer (C) and mark it on your answer sheet.

1.

2.

GO ON TO THE NEXT PAGE

3.

4.

5.

6.

GO ON TO THE NEXT PAGE

TEST 3

PART 2

Directions: You will hear a question or statement and three responses spoken in English. They will not be printed in your test book and will be spoken only one time. Select the best response to the question or statement and mark the letter (A), (B), or (C) on your answer sheet.

7. Mark your answer on your answer sheet.

8. Mark your answer on your answer sheet.

9. Mark your answer on your answer sheet.

10. Mark your answer on your answer sheet.

11. Mark your answer on your answer sheet.

12. Mark your answer on your answer sheet.

13. Mark your answer on your answer sheet.

14. Mark your answer on your answer sheet.

15. Mark your answer on your answer sheet.

16. Mark your answer on your answer sheet.

17. Mark your answer on your answer sheet.

18. Mark your answer on your answer sheet.

19. Mark your answer on your answer sheet.

20. Mark your answer on your answer sheet.

21. Mark your answer on your answer sheet.

22. Mark your answer on your answer sheet.

23. Mark your answer on your answer sheet.

24. Mark your answer on your answer sheet.

25. Mark your answer on your answer sheet.

26. Mark your answer on your answer sheet.

27. Mark your answer on your answer sheet.

28. Mark your answer on your answer sheet.

29. Mark your answer on your answer sheet.

30. Mark your answer on your answer sheet.

31. Mark your answer on your answer sheet.

PART 3

Directions: You will hear some conversations between two or more people. You will be asked to answer three questions about what the speakers say in each conversation. Select the best response to each question and mark the letter (A), (B), (C), or (D) on your answer sheet. The conversations will not be printed in your test book and will be spoken only one time.

32. What does the company most likely produce?

(A) Print advertisements
(B) Television shows
(C) Computer parts
(D) Musical instruments

33. What department will the man work in?

(A) Accounting
(B) Legal
(C) Human resources
(D) Security

34. What does the man like about his work area?

(A) It is conveniently located.
(B) It has a good view.
(C) It is quiet.
(D) It is nicely decorated.

35. What is the conversation mainly about?

(A) A room reservation
(B) A canceled event
(C) A restaurant recommendation
(D) A misplaced item

36. What does the man need to provide?

(A) A security deposit
(B) A revised schedule
(C) A form of identification
(D) A business address

37. What do the visitors ask for?

(A) A refund
(B) Better lighting
(C) Menu options
(D) More chairs

38. Where does the conversation most likely take place?

(A) At a shopping mall
(B) At a theater
(C) In a sports stadium
(D) On a train

39. Why does the woman say, "The football championship is this afternoon"?

(A) To extend an invitation
(B) To offer encouragement
(C) To give an explanation
(D) To request a schedule change

40. What does the man say he needs to purchase?

(A) Tickets
(B) Clothes
(C) Food
(D) Furniture

41. What problem does the man mention?

(A) Some products are damaged.
(B) Some equipment is out of stock.
(C) A vehicle has broken down.
(D) A delivery error has occurred.

42. What does the woman say is planned for Friday?

(A) A product launch
(B) An inspection
(C) A cooking class
(D) An interview

43. What does the man say he will do?

(A) Transfer a call
(B) Issue a refund
(C) Provide a warranty
(D) Visit a business

GO ON TO THE NEXT PAGE

44. Where do the speakers most likely work?

(A) At a law office
(B) At a supermarket
(C) At a medical clinic
(D) At a recreation center

45. What are the speakers mainly discussing?

(A) A marketing campaign
(B) A new product
(C) Some budget cuts
(D) Some survey results

46. What does the woman imply when she says, "That would require significant revisions to our scheduling process"?

(A) She doubts a change will be implemented.
(B) She thinks more staff should be hired.
(C) She needs more time to make a decision.
(D) She believes some data is incorrect.

47. Why did the woman miss a meeting?

(A) She was not feeling well.
(B) She was on a business trip.
(C) She was speaking with a client.
(D) She did not receive the invitation.

48. What is the woman confused about?

(A) The details of an assignment
(B) A reimbursement process
(C) The terms of a contract
(D) A travel itinerary

49. According to the man, what should the woman do?

(A) Reset the password for her computer
(B) Talk to the organizer of the meeting
(C) Consult the electronic version of a document
(D) Research the history of an account

50. What is the woman an expert in?

(A) Gardening
(B) Nutrition
(C) Appliance repair
(D) Fitness training

51. What does the woman recommend?

(A) Substituting ingredients
(B) Using appropriate tools
(C) Changing an exercise routine
(D) Scheduling regular maintenance

52. According to the woman, where can listeners find more information?

(A) On a television show
(B) On a Web site
(C) In a magazine
(D) In a book

53. What does the woman say about the man's job performance?

(A) He is respected by his colleagues.
(B) He always meets his deadlines.
(C) He has good ideas for new projects.
(D) He has increased company profits.

54. What does the woman ask the man to do?

(A) Attend a trade show
(B) Join a leadership council
(C) Mentor a colleague
(D) Accept a new position

55. When will the speakers meet again?

(A) Tomorrow
(B) Next week
(C) Next month
(D) Next quarter

56. What does the man ask the women about?

(A) The types of projects assigned
(B) The backgrounds of the applicants
(C) The status of training materials
(D) The location of an orientation

57. What does the man say about last year's internship program?

(A) Some new products were developed.
(B) Some information was unclear.
(C) There were not enough supplies.
(D) There were a large number of applicants.

58. What does the man say he is pleased about?

(A) The summer schedule
(B) The careful planning
(C) The deadline extension
(D) The approval process

---

59. What type of business does the woman work for?

(A) A moving company
(B) A real estate agency
(C) An insurance firm
(D) An equipment rental service

60. What is the woman concerned about?

(A) Shipping delays
(B) New regulations
(C) An increase in competition
(D) A shortage of staff

61. What does the woman emphasize about her company?

(A) The affordable prices
(B) The number of branch offices
(C) The user-friendly Web site
(D) The customer service

Catering Company	Cost
Café Delight	$1,250
Corner Deli	$1,400
Golden Eagle	$950
Star Restaurant	$850

62. What type of event are the speakers discussing?

(A) A shareholders' meeting
(B) A press conference
(C) A job fair
(D) A product demonstration

63. What problem did the woman experience with one of the restaurants?

(A) An unhelpful staff member
(B) A poorly cooked meal
(C) A billing error
(D) A delivery delay

64. Look at the graphic. How much will the lunch most likely cost?

(A) $1,250
(B) $1,400
(C) $950
(D) $850

GO ON TO THE NEXT PAGE

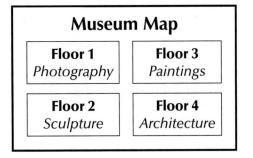

Museum Map

| **Floor 1** *Photography* | **Floor 3** *Paintings* |
| **Floor 2** *Sculpture* | **Floor 4** *Architecture* |

65. Look at the graphic. On which floor will the man meet his friends?

   (A) Floor 1
   (B) Floor 2
   (C) Floor 3
   (D) Floor 4

66. What will happen at the museum this summer?

   (A) A workshop will be offered.
   (B) A special exhibit will open.
   (C) Concerts will be held in the garden.
   (D) Some galleries will be renovated.

67. Why does the woman suggest using the stairs at the back of the museum?

   (A) They are nearby.
   (B) They offer a good view.
   (C) They were recently added.
   (D) They are not crowded.

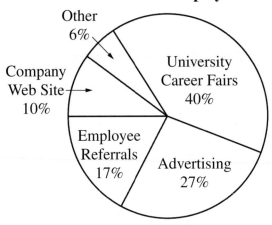

How Do We Find Employees?

68. What does the woman want to do?

   (A) Make travel arrangements
   (B) Revise a budget
   (C) Change recruiting tactics
   (D) Give a lecture

69. Look at the graphic. Which method does the man suggest using?

   (A) University career fairs
   (B) Advertising
   (C) Employee referrals
   (D) Company Web site

70. What does the woman suggest the man do?

   (A) Design a questionnaire
   (B) Renew a contract
   (C) Work with a colleague
   (D) Interview a job candidate

Directions: You will hear some talks given by a single speaker. You will be asked to answer three questions about what the speaker says in each talk. Select the best response to each question and mark the letter (A), (B), (C), or (D) on your answer sheet. The talks will not be printed in your test book and will be spoken only one time.

71. At which event is the announcement being made?

(A) A book fair
(B) A product launch
(C) A technology conference
(D) A charity fundraiser

72. According to the speaker, what can some listeners do tomorrow?

(A) Go on a tour
(B) Attend an opening ceremony
(C) Participate in a focus group
(D) Win a prize

73. What are the listeners instructed to do?

(A) Use an alternate entrance
(B) Register in advance
(C) Complete a survey
(D) Meet at a designated location

74. What product does Castillo manufacture?

(A) Jewelry
(B) Clothing
(C) Art supplies
(D) Backpacks

75. Why does the speaker say, "Just look at the color selection in these samples"?

(A) To introduce a new manufacturing technique
(B) To assign a task
(C) To express disappointment
(D) To support a decision

76. What will Hae-Rim do?

(A) Present financial information
(B) Share competitor data
(C) Analyze survey results
(D) Introduce advertising layouts

77. Who most likely is the speaker?

(A) An investment banker
(B) A city official
(C) A food scientist
(D) A restaurant manager

78. According to the speaker, what will happen next week?

(A) Some new equipment will be installed.
(B) A corporate office will relocate.
(C) New menu items will be available.
(D) Seasonal employees will begin work.

79. What does the speaker warn listeners about?

(A) Preparing orders carefully
(B) Wearing proper attire
(C) Recording hours accurately
(D) Taking inventory daily

80. Why is the speaker calling?

(A) To register for a training session
(B) To request help with a project
(C) To book a meeting room
(D) To get updated customer information

81. What does the speaker imply when she says, "it wasn't my idea"?

(A) She knows a change is inconvenient.
(B) She thinks a colleague deserves credit.
(C) She would like the listener's opinion.
(D) She is going to explain a new procedure.

82. What does the speaker ask the listener to do?

(A) Order business cards
(B) Check a mailbox
(C) Revise a report
(D) Reserve a booth

GO ON TO THE NEXT PAGE

83. What will the company do beginning on June 1 ?

(A) Accept reservations online
(B) Provide service to a new location
(C) Offer a customer loyalty program
(D) Lower its express shipping rates

84. According to the speaker, what must customers do in order to ship a vehicle?

(A) Show proof of ownership
(B) Provide an extra set of keys
(C) Purchase additional insurance
(D) Get a mechanical inspection

85. What does the speaker indicate about the call?

(A) It will be redirected to a different department.
(B) It will be answered in the order in which it was received.
(C) It may be several minutes until a representative answers.
(D) It may be recorded for future use.

86. Who is the intended audience for the talk?

(A) Theater patrons
(B) Costume makers
(C) Ticket sellers
(D) Stage musicians

87. What does the speaker mention about the play?

(A) It is very long.
(B) It is set in the past.
(C) There are many characters.
(D) There is a waiting list for tickets.

88. What will take place in five weeks?

(A) A photography session
(B) A dinner reception
(C) A fashion show
(D) A dress rehearsal

89. What was the speaker supposed to do this morning?

(A) Interview a job applicant
(B) Attend a meeting
(C) Pick up a client
(D) Lead a tour group

90. What transportation problem does the speaker mention?

(A) A road has been closed.
(B) A bridge is under construction.
(C) A train service is unavailable.
(D) A flight has been delayed.

91. What does the speaker suggest?

(A) Inviting other colleagues
(B) Posting a notice
(C) Holding a phone conference
(D) Having lunch together

92. What industry does the speaker work in?

(A) Renewable energy
(B) Computer technology
(C) Publishing
(D) Real estate

93. What does the speaker imply when he says, "hundreds of businesses have signed up"?

(A) He is worried about meeting client demands.
(B) He expects an industry to start changing.
(C) The listeners should choose his company.
(D) The listeners will receive a list of contacts.

94. What will the listeners see in the video?

(A) A virtual tour
(B) An award-acceptance speech
(C) Product features
(D) Installation instructions

Feedback Survey

Cleanliness	★★★★ 4 stars
Location	★★★★ 4 stars
Staff friendliness	★★★★★ 5 stars
Cost	★★★ 3 stars

95. Who is the message most likely for?

(A) A fitness instructor
(B) A data analyst
(C) A gym member
(D) A marketing expert

96. What does the speaker say he has e-mailed the listener?

(A) A discount voucher
(B) Driving directions
(C) A fitness magazine
(D) Class schedules

97. Look at the graphic. Which category does the speaker request more information about?

(A) Cleanliness
(B) Location
(C) Staff friendliness
(D) Cost

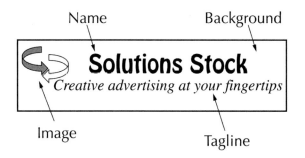

Name   Background

Image   Tagline

98. Where is the talk most likely taking place?

(A) At a business class
(B) At a software training session
(C) At a department meeting
(D) At a client presentation

99. Look at the graphic. Which part of the logo does the speaker discuss first?

(A) The name
(B) The background
(C) The image
(D) The tagline

100. What will the listeners do next?

(A) Break into small groups
(B) Write down some ideas
(C) Read an article
(D) Check a Web site

This is the end of the Listening test.

토익˙정기시험
기출문제집

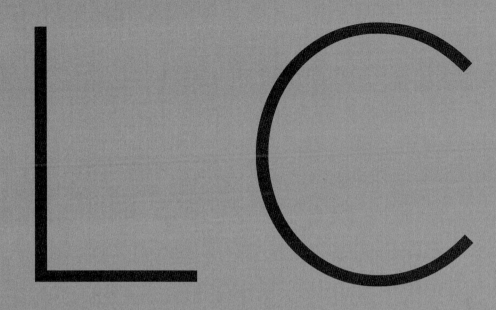

LC

기출 TEST

04

LISTENING TEST

In the Listening test, you will be asked to demonstrate how well you understand spoken English. The entire Listening test will last approximately 45 minutes. There are four parts, and directions are given for each part. You must mark your answers on the separate answer sheet. Do not write your answers in your test book.

PART 1

Directions: For each question in this part, you will hear four statements about a picture in your test book. When you hear the statements, you must select the one statement that best describes what you see in the picture. Then find the number of the question on your answer sheet and mark your answer. The statements will not be printed in your test book and will be spoken only one time.

Statement (C), "They're sitting at a table," is the best description of the picture, so you should select answer (C) and mark it on your answer sheet.

1.

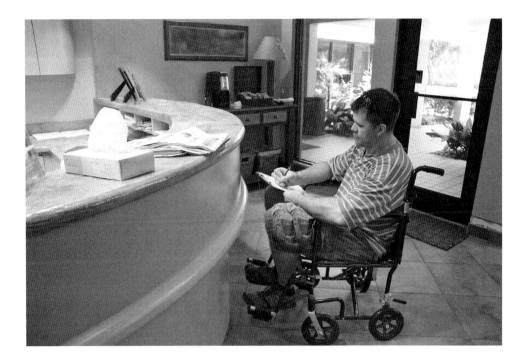

2.

GO ON TO THE NEXT PAGE

3.

4.

5.

6.

GO ON TO THE NEXT PAGE

PART 2

Directions: You will hear a question or statement and three responses spoken in English. They will not be printed in your test book and will be spoken only one time. Select the best response to the question or statement and mark the letter (A), (B), or (C) on your answer sheet.

7. Mark your answer on your answer sheet.

8. Mark your answer on your answer sheet.

9. Mark your answer on your answer sheet.

10. Mark your answer on your answer sheet.

11. Mark your answer on your answer sheet.

12. Mark your answer on your answer sheet.

13. Mark your answer on your answer sheet.

14. Mark your answer on your answer sheet.

15. Mark your answer on your answer sheet.

16. Mark your answer on your answer sheet.

17. Mark your answer on your answer sheet.

18. Mark your answer on your answer sheet.

19. Mark your answer on your answer sheet.

20. Mark your answer on your answer sheet.

21. Mark your answer on your answer sheet.

22. Mark your answer on your answer sheet.

23. Mark your answer on your answer sheet.

24. Mark your answer on your answer sheet.

25. Mark your answer on your answer sheet.

26. Mark your answer on your answer sheet.

27. Mark your answer on your answer sheet.

28. Mark your answer on your answer sheet.

29. Mark your answer on your answer sheet.

30. Mark your answer on your answer sheet.

31. Mark your answer on your answer sheet.

PART 3

Directions: You will hear some conversations between two or more people. You will be asked to answer three questions about what the speakers say in each conversation. Select the best response to each question and mark the letter (A), (B), (C), or (D) on your answer sheet. The conversations will not be printed in your test book and will be spoken only one time.

32. What are the speakers discussing?

(A) An arrival time
(B) A seat assignment
(C) A ticket price
(D) A travel policy

33. Where is the conversation taking place?

(A) In a parking garage
(B) At a car rental agency
(C) On a train
(D) In a baggage claim area

34. What does the man say he will do?

(A) Show his identification card
(B) Gather his luggage
(C) Ask for a refund
(D) Speak with a supervisor

35. What most likely is the woman's job?

(A) Lab technician
(B) Receptionist
(C) Pharmacist
(D) Doctor

36. What does the woman want to change?

(A) The quantity of items in an order
(B) The location of a seminar
(C) The time of an appointment
(D) A payment schedule

37. What will the man do next?

(A) Update his calendar
(B) Submit his medical records
(C) Review an invoice
(D) Prepare an agenda

38. Where do the speakers work?

(A) At a phone company
(B) At a retail store
(C) At a hotel
(D) At a theater

39. What does the woman tell the man about?

(A) A new restaurant
(B) A music performance
(C) A group discount
(D) A maintenance request

40. What will the man do after lunch?

(A) Listen to his phone messages
(B) Send a confirmation e-mail
(C) Return some tickets
(D) Go to the woman's office

41. What does the man ask the woman to do?

(A) Place an order
(B) Recommend a product
(C) Explain a feature
(D) Reduce a price

42. What does the man say he will do with a video camera?

(A) Document his travels
(B) Use it for a class
(C) Record staff meetings
(D) Make a commercial

43. What does the woman say about the Sepler 83 ?

(A) It has a rechargeable battery.
(B) It has positive customer reviews.
(C) It is a new model.
(D) It is easy to use.

GO ON TO THE NEXT PAGE

44. Where do the speakers most likely work?

    (A) At a medical clinic
    (B) At a catering company
    (C) At a convenience store
    (D) At a manufacturing plant

45. Why does the woman say, "This isn't the first time this has happened"?

    (A) She is frustrated with a vendor.
    (B) She does not agree with an idea.
    (C) She knows how to solve a problem.
    (D) She wants the listener to be more cautious.

46. What will the woman most likely do next?

    (A) Check some equipment
    (B) Speak with a manager
    (C) Load a vehicle
    (D) Go to a store

47. What is Dorota's field of study?

    (A) Economics
    (B) Marketing
    (C) Chemistry
    (D) Accounting

48. What does the man want to review with Dorota?

    (A) Payroll procedures
    (B) Safety precautions
    (C) Admission requirements
    (D) A building directory

49. Why has a training been postponed?

    (A) A computer server is down.
    (B) A facility has been closed.
    (C) Some materials are missing.
    (D) Transportation is unavailable.

50. What problem does the woman mention?

    (A) An invoice is incorrect.
    (B) A window is broken.
    (C) A job is incomplete.
    (D) A water pipe is leaking.

51. According to the man, what caused the problem?

    (A) Poor maintenance
    (B) Weather conditions
    (C) Low-quality products
    (D) Inexperienced workers

52. What does the man say he will do right away?

    (A) Send a warranty
    (B) Contact a supervisor
    (C) Pick up some supplies
    (D) Adjust a schedule

53. What type of business is the woman calling?

    (A) A library
    (B) A computer store
    (C) A fitness center
    (D) A magazine company

54. What does the man suggest?

    (A) Replacing a membership card
    (B) Calling back later
    (C) Purchasing an online subscription
    (D) Updating contact information

55. What does the woman ask about?

    (A) A discount
    (B) A refund policy
    (C) Overnight delivery
    (D) Hours of operation

56. What are the speakers discussing?

(A) A budget
(B) A client survey
(C) A new employee
(D) A presentation

57. What type of company do the speakers work for?

(A) A financial-planning business
(B) An insurance company
(C) A marketing firm
(D) A law office

58. What does the woman say should be emphasized?

(A) Creating innovative products
(B) Expanding the customer base
(C) Building an effective team
(D) Reducing expenses

59. What is the woman preparing for?

(A) A training session
(B) A job interview
(C) A safety inspection
(D) A product review

60. What does the man imply when he says, "I finished my project early"?

(A) He wants feedback on a task.
(B) He has time to offer assistance.
(C) He would like to leave for the day.
(D) He thinks he deserves a promotion.

61. What will the man most likely do next?

(A) Postpone a meeting
(B) Follow up on a request
(C) Check a piece of equipment
(D) Review a policy

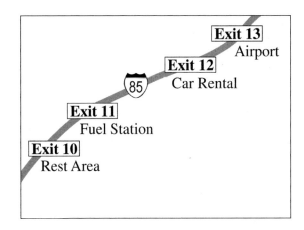

62. What are the speakers concerned about?

(A) Finding a parking space
(B) Missing a flight
(C) Paying an additional charge
(D) Avoiding heavy traffic

63. Look at the graphic. Which exit does the woman tell the man to take?

(A) Exit 10
(B) Exit 11
(C) Exit 12
(D) Exit 13

64. What does the man say he hopes to do?

(A) Buy some food
(B) Pick up a map
(C) Make a phone call
(D) Purchase souvenirs

GO ON TO THE NEXT PAGE

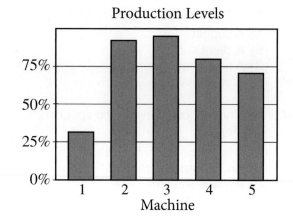

https://www.reviewyourstay.com

Sentora Hotel review

Location ★★★★★

Hotel facilities ★★★★

Guest services ★★

Room appearance ★★

Production Levels

65. What does the woman say she is worried about?

(A) Exceeding a budget
(B) Hosting a conference
(C) Losing customers
(D) Passing an inspection

66. Look at the graphic. Which category will be discussed in the next staff meeting?

(A) Location
(B) Hotel facilities
(C) Guest services
(D) Room appearance

67. What does the man suggest doing?

(A) Buying new equipment
(B) Changing a reservation
(C) Providing a discount
(D) Hiring a consultant

68. What industry do the speakers work in?

(A) Car repair
(B) Appliance sales
(C) Food manufacturing
(D) Packaging design

69. Look at the graphic. Which machine is being discussed?

(A) Machine 1
(B) Machine 2
(C) Machine 3
(D) Machine 4

70. What does the woman say she will do next?

(A) Taste some samples
(B) Request some maintenance
(C) Print another report
(D) Check some specifications

PART 4

Directions: You will hear some talks given by a single speaker. You will be asked to answer three questions about what the speaker says in each talk. Select the best response to each question and mark the letter (A), (B), (C), or (D) on your answer sheet. The talks will not be printed in your test book and will be spoken only one time.

71. What does the speaker announce?

(A) A company merger
(B) A schedule change
(C) A revised travel policy
(D) A new contract

72. According to the speaker, what has Skycloud Aviation requested?

(A) Extra luggage space
(B) In-flight entertainment
(C) Movable seats
(D) Wireless Internet technology

73. What are listeners asked to do?

(A) Update their calendars
(B) Discuss a project plan
(C) Submit expense reports
(D) Contact some clients

74. Why is the speaker calling?

(A) To schedule a meeting
(B) To ask for an e-mail address
(C) To provide an invoice number
(D) To review employee training plans

75. What does the speaker mean when she says, "there's a team meeting this afternoon"?

(A) She will be late to another meeting.
(B) Materials need to be prepared.
(C) A staff member is busy.
(D) A project has already been completed.

76. What will the speaker do tomorrow?

(A) Meet with Mariko
(B) Attend a party for Angelo
(C) Finish a proposal
(D) Print a set of documents

77. What type of business is Kendris?

(A) A new car dealership
(B) An auto parts manufacturer
(C) An electronics importer
(D) A local marketing firm

78. According to the speaker, what is special about a new product?

(A) It is the least expensive on the market.
(B) It is endorsed by a celebrity.
(C) It can be customized.
(D) It is made to last longer than others.

79. According to the speaker, what will take place in August?

(A) An industry trade show
(B) A company merger
(C) A radio interview
(D) A sporting event

80. What is available at the back of the room?

(A) A list of materials
(B) Refreshments
(C) Protective clothing
(D) Name tags

81. What does the speaker imply when he says, "Space is limited"?

(A) A class will meet in a bigger room.
(B) A building will be renovated.
(C) A mistake should be addressed.
(D) A decision should be made soon.

82. What will the listeners do next?

(A) Pay a materials fee
(B) Watch a demonstration
(C) View sample artwork
(D) Meet a famous artist

GO ON TO THE NEXT PAGE

83. What industry does Janet Colthrup work in?

(A) Event planning
(B) Accounting
(C) Tourism
(D) Interior design

84. What will Janet Colthrup discuss?

(A) Tips for starting a business
(B) Strategies for international trade
(C) Modern home-decorating styles
(D) Effective speech-writing techniques

85. What does the speaker request that listeners do?

(A) Take a handout before they leave
(B) Submit their questions in writing
(C) Move to the empty seats in the front
(D) Split into small discussion groups

86. What event took place last weekend?

(A) An art exhibit
(B) An opening ceremony
(C) An outdoor concert
(D) An awards dinner

87. Why is the city raising money?

(A) To build a park
(B) To improve roads
(C) To open a museum
(D) To create a monument

88. Why was the event rescheduled?

(A) Ticket sales were low.
(B) A location was unavailable.
(C) A celebrity guest canceled.
(D) The weather was bad.

89. Why has the tour bus stopped?

(A) To let the passengers out for shopping
(B) To purchase fuel
(C) To allow the guide to point out a view
(D) To pay a toll

90. According to the speaker, why is Fremont historically important?

(A) It used to be a center of trade.
(B) It is the oldest town along the river.
(C) An important battle took place there.
(D) A famous author was born there.

91. What will the tour group do next?

(A) Watch a documentary
(B) Take a group picture
(C) Board a boat
(D) Have lunch

92. What is the Health Monitor?

(A) A television program
(B) A wearable device
(C) A medical Web site
(D) A fitness center

93. What does the speaker mean when she says, "Who wants to do that"?

(A) A task is inconvenient.
(B) A project requires more volunteers.
(C) An event is no longer popular.
(D) An application period has begun.

94. Why are listeners encouraged to act soon?

(A) Some stores are closing.
(B) Tickets are almost sold out.
(C) A product is temporarily discounted.
(D) A deadline has been changed.

July 3–Afternoon	Speaker
Session 1	Maria Garcia
Session 2	Klaus Bauer
Session 3	Naoko Ito
Session 4	Jeff Harper

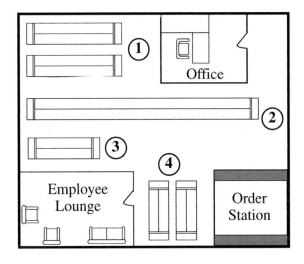

95. Who is the conference intended for?

(A) Video-game developers
(B) Photojournalists
(C) Health-care professionals
(D) Automobile engineers

96. Look at the graphic. Which session has been changed?

(A) Session 1
(B) Session 2
(C) Session 3
(D) Session 4

97. How can listeners enter a contest?

(A) By submitting a work sample
(B) By providing some feedback
(C) By subscribing to a newsletter
(D) By moderating at a session

98. Why is a change being made?

(A) To improve efficiency
(B) To follow a safety procedure
(C) To make some repairs
(D) To prepare for new hires

99. Look at the graphic. Where are the new shelves located?

(A) Area 1
(B) Area 2
(C) Area 3
(D) Area 4

100. What does the speaker say listeners can find in the office?

(A) Some work badges
(B) Some equipment manuals
(C) A sign-up sheet
(D) An employee handbook

This is the end of the Listening test.

토익® 정기시험
기출문제집

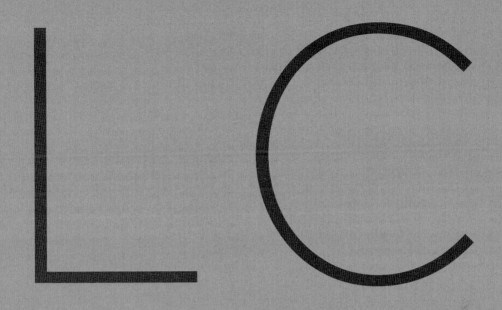

LC

기출 TEST

05

LISTENING TEST

In the Listening test, you will be asked to demonstrate how well you understand spoken English. The entire Listening test will last approximately 45 minutes. There are four parts, and directions are given for each part. You must mark your answers on the separate answer sheet. Do not write your answers in your test book.

PART 1

Directions: For each question in this part, you will hear four statements about a picture in your test book. When you hear the statements, you must select the one statement that best describes what you see in the picture. Then find the number of the question on your answer sheet and mark your answer. The statements will not be printed in your test book and will be spoken only one time.

Statement (C), "They're sitting at a table," is the best description of the picture, so you should select answer (C) and mark it on your answer sheet.

1.

2.

GO ON TO THE NEXT PAGE

3.

4.

5.

6.

GO ON TO THE NEXT PAGE

PART 2

Directions: You will hear a question or statement and three responses spoken in English. They will not be printed in your test book and will be spoken only one time. Select the best response to the question or statement and mark the letter (A), (B), or (C) on your answer sheet.

7. Mark your answer on your answer sheet.

8. Mark your answer on your answer sheet.

9. Mark your answer on your answer sheet.

10. Mark your answer on your answer sheet.

11. Mark your answer on your answer sheet.

12. Mark your answer on your answer sheet.

13. Mark your answer on your answer sheet.

14. Mark your answer on your answer sheet.

15. Mark your answer on your answer sheet.

16. Mark your answer on your answer sheet.

17. Mark your answer on your answer sheet.

18. Mark your answer on your answer sheet.

19. Mark your answer on your answer sheet.

20. Mark your answer on your answer sheet.

21. Mark your answer on your answer sheet.

22. Mark your answer on your answer sheet.

23. Mark your answer on your answer sheet.

24. Mark your answer on your answer sheet.

25. Mark your answer on your answer sheet.

26. Mark your answer on your answer sheet.

27. Mark your answer on your answer sheet.

28. Mark your answer on your answer sheet.

29. Mark your answer on your answer sheet.

30. Mark your answer on your answer sheet.

31. Mark your answer on your answer sheet.

PART 3

Directions: You will hear some conversations between two or more people. You will be asked to answer three questions about what the speakers say in each conversation. Select the best response to each question and mark the letter (A), (B), (C), or (D) on your answer sheet. The conversations will not be printed in your test book and will be spoken only one time.

32. Who most likely is the man?

    (A) A Web-site designer
    (B) A truck driver
    (C) A factory worker
    (D) A customer service representative

33. What is the woman trying to do?

    (A) Add an item to an order
    (B) Change a delivery location
    (C) Return a damaged product
    (D) Correct a billing error

34. What does the man offer to do?

    (A) Reimburse a purchase
    (B) Contact a shipping agent
    (C) Check a price
    (D) Expedite a shipment

35. What will the man do on Monday?

    (A) Attend a seminar
    (B) Graduate from school
    (C) Start a new position
    (D) Receive an award

36. Why does the man say he is busy?

    (A) He is moving into a different office.
    (B) He is meeting with some clients.
    (C) He has an upcoming business trip.
    (D) He has a project deadline.

37. What does the woman offer to do?

    (A) Review an expense report
    (B) Arrange a company celebration
    (C) Introduce the man to a colleague
    (D) Provide the man with supplies

38. What has the man just finished doing?

    (A) Negotiating a contract
    (B) Repairing a television
    (C) Producing an advertisement
    (D) Interviewing a job candidate

39. What does the woman imply when she says, "Rashid has worked in television for years"?

    (A) Rashid's opinion would be valuable.
    (B) Rashid's résumé is out of date.
    (C) Rashid should receive a promotion.
    (D) Rashid wants to change careers.

40. What does the man say he is concerned about?

    (A) Staying under budget
    (B) Impressing a client
    (C) Arriving on time to a meeting
    (D) Satisfying a technical requirement

41. According to the woman, what is taking place next week?

    (A) A career fair
    (B) A retirement celebration
    (C) A promotional event
    (D) An anniversary party

42. Why does the woman say, "have you ever met Mr. Kato"?

    (A) To point out a mistake
    (B) To introduce a colleague
    (C) To recommend a staff member
    (D) To complain about a service

43. What does the woman offer to do?

    (A) Review some slides
    (B) Pay for a delivery
    (C) Contact a client
    (D) Call a restaurant

GO ON TO THE NEXT PAGE

44. Why is the man calling the woman?

   (A) To congratulate her
   (B) To apologize to her
   (C) To set up an interview
   (D) To organize a client visit

45. What do the speakers say about James Tanaka?

   (A) He has worked overseas.
   (B) He is very talented.
   (C) He is familiar with the company policies.
   (D) He is easy to work with.

46. What does the woman promise to do tomorrow?

   (A) Revise some documents
   (B) E-mail some customers
   (C) Create a training course
   (D) Give feedback to a colleague

___

47. What are the speakers discussing?

   (A) Invitations for a library fund-raiser
   (B) Applications for a construction permit
   (C) Design plans for a new building
   (D) Membership requirements for patrons

48. What is the man concerned about?

   (A) How to lower costs
   (B) When to hold an event
   (C) Who will be in charge of training
   (D) Where a room will be located

49. What does the man say he will do this afternoon?

   (A) Confirm some information
   (B) Purchase some equipment
   (C) Reserve a meeting space
   (D) Write a book review

___

50. Why was the woman disappointed with a hotel?

   (A) It was far from the city center.
   (B) It was crowded with guests.
   (C) The staff were inattentive.
   (D) The rooms were small.

51. What does the man say he will do?

   (A) Call a taxi
   (B) Print out a ticket
   (C) Check an advertisement
   (D) Contact a colleague

52. What does the woman request?

   (A) An extra key
   (B) A reimbursement
   (C) A city map
   (D) A room upgrade

___

53. Why is the woman traveling to Paris?

   (A) To visit a friend
   (B) To attend a meeting
   (C) To watch a performance
   (D) To inspect a store

54. What does the man explain to the woman?

   (A) How to avoid a delay
   (B) How to reset an electronic device
   (C) How to fill out some paperwork
   (D) How to retrieve a ticket

55. What does the man suggest?

   (A) Going to the train station together
   (B) Searching online for an address
   (C) Inviting another colleague
   (D) Submitting some travel receipts

___

56. What are the speakers mainly discussing?

    (A) A computer malfunction
    (B) A company policy
    (C) A financial report
    (D) A recent holiday

57. Why does the man say, "What if I need to contact my bank"?

    (A) To explain why he is concerned
    (B) To suggest revising a budget
    (C) To request some contact information
    (D) To ask for a deadline extension

58. According to the woman, what complaint has been made about some employees?

    (A) They need technical training.
    (B) They work inconsistent hours.
    (C) They waste work time.
    (D) They are disorganized.

59. What is the woman invited to do?

    (A) Join coworkers for lunch
    (B) Travel to a conference
    (C) Lead a seminar
    (D) Interview for a job

60. What does the woman say she is concerned about?

    (A) Not being qualified
    (B) Not having enough time
    (C) Losing a reserved seat
    (D) Missing a call

61. What will the woman most likely do next?

    (A) Request a refund
    (B) Open an account
    (C) Speak with a manager
    (D) Ask for a menu

62. What does the woman want to buy?

    (A) Kitchen appliances
    (B) Cooking supplies
    (C) Wall decorations
    (D) Dining furniture

63. Why will the woman receive a discount?

    (A) She is purchasing a large quantity.
    (B) She lives close to the store.
    (C) Some of the products are damaged.
    (D) The store is having a sale.

64. What does the woman say will happen next month?

    (A) A business will open.
    (B) An inspection will begin.
    (C) An invoice will be sent.
    (D) A road will be closed.

GO ON TO THE NEXT PAGE

Error Code	Problem
☐ E-1	Dirty lens
☐ E-2	No flash
☐ E-3	Low battery
☐ E-4	Memory card full

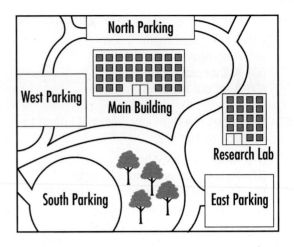

65. Who most likely is the woman?

(A) A workshop instructor
(B) A store clerk
(C) An electrician
(D) A product designer

66. Look at the graphic. Which error code is the camera displaying?

(A) E-1
(B) E-2
(C) E-3
(D) E-4

67. What will the woman most likely do next?

(A) Replace an item
(B) Take a photograph
(C) Read a manual
(D) Show some slides

68. Look at the graphic. Which parking area will be closed?

(A) North
(B) East
(C) South
(D) West

69. What is the woman concerned about?

(A) Building security access
(B) Parking fees
(C) Road conditions
(D) Heavy traffic

70. What does the man say the company will do?

(A) Reimburse employees
(B) Offer a shuttle service
(C) Provide maps
(D) Distribute electronic badges

PART 4

Directions: You will hear some talks given by a single speaker. You will be asked to answer three questions about what the speaker says in each talk. Select the best response to each question and mark the letter (A), (B), (C), or (D) on your answer sheet. The talks will not be printed in your test book and will be spoken only one time.

71. Where does the woman work?

    (A) At a furniture store
    (B) At a bank
    (C) At a law office
    (D) At a construction company

72. What problem does the woman mention?

    (A) A machine is broken.
    (B) A contract has not been signed.
    (C) A price list is incorrect.
    (D) An item is out of stock.

73. Why does the woman ask the man to call her back?

    (A) To verify his credit card number
    (B) To confirm a color choice
    (C) To provide his e-mail address
    (D) To get directions to a building site

74. Where is the talk most likely taking place?

    (A) At a software development company
    (B) At a medical office
    (C) At a moving company
    (D) At a training institute

75. What will happen on October tenth?

    (A) A new manager will join the team.
    (B) A staff member will be out of the office.
    (C) A business will move to a new location.
    (D) A new computer system will be put in place.

76. What will the listeners do next?

    (A) Schedule appointments
    (B) View a product demonstration
    (C) Have a discussion
    (D) Relocate some files

77. What event is being discussed?

    (A) A city tour
    (B) A hotel renovation
    (C) A company anniversary
    (D) A professional conference

78. What are listeners reminded to do?

    (A) Sign up early
    (B) Bring a camera
    (C) Check identification
    (D) Read a manual

79. What can listeners do in the afternoon?

    (A) Attend presentations
    (B) Watch a video
    (C) Meet city officials
    (D) Visit museums

80. What is the speaker planning?

    (A) A fund-raising party
    (B) A welcome reception
    (C) An award ceremony
    (D) An annual picnic

81. What does the speaker imply when she says, "35 people have accepted the invitation"?

    (A) She thinks changing a date would be difficult.
    (B) She forgot to notify some people about an event.
    (C) The current venue is too small.
    (D) A ticket price is too high.

82. What does the speaker ask the listener to do?

    (A) Update a database
    (B) Prepare some name tags
    (C) Help select a speaker
    (D) Make some phone calls

GO ON TO THE NEXT PAGE

83. What is the speaker mainly discussing?

   (A) A revised work schedule
   (B) New fitness equipment
   (C) Opportunities for promotion
   (D) Free exercise classes

84. What are the listeners asked to do?

   (A) Read about some products
   (B) Submit hours of availability
   (C) Contact a supplier
   (D) Fill out an application

85. According to the speaker, what will occur next week?

   (A) A holiday sale
   (B) A store opening
   (C) A training session
   (D) A trade show

86. What does the speaker want to talk about?

   (A) Working on a different project
   (B) Modifying an agenda
   (C) Moving to a new office space
   (D) Arranging a client visit

87. Why does the speaker say, "you are right next to the break room"?

   (A) To suggest that a location is undesirable
   (B) To propose taking a break
   (C) To turn down a colleague's invitation
   (D) To ask about a convenient place to meet

88. What does the speaker say will take place on Monday?

   (A) A sales presentation
   (B) A department orientation
   (C) A facility tour
   (D) A computer installation

89. Where do the listeners most likely work?

   (A) At a clothing factory
   (B) At an electronics shop
   (C) At an art museum
   (D) At a shoe store

90. Who is Jacqueline Porter?

   (A) A store clerk
   (B) A corporate trainer
   (C) A clothing designer
   (D) An advertising executive

91. What does the speaker remind listeners to do?

   (A) Turn off mobile phones
   (B) Sign a receipt
   (C) Complete a survey
   (D) Put up a display

Tuesday Schedule		
9:00	Board meeting	Room 223
9:30	Marketing meeting	Auditorium
9:30	Product development videoconference	Room 407
11:00	All-staff meeting	Cafeteria

92. What happened last night?

   (A) Some servers were delivered.
   (B) The electricity went out.
   (C) A Web site was launched.
   (D) Some keys were lost.

93. Look at the graphic. Which room will the speaker go to next?

   (A) Room 223
   (B) Auditorium
   (C) Room 407
   (D) Cafeteria

94. According to the speaker, what will Li Wei do?

   (A) Lead a repair crew
   (B) Test out some products
   (C) Install some software
   (D) Answer a telephone

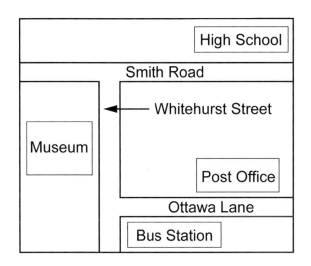

BLOOM AIRLINES

To: **Los Angeles**
Flight: **B1205**
Gate: **22C**   Seat: **8D**
Departure Time: **9:15**

95. Who gave a press conference today?

   (A) A civil engineer
   (B) A local student
   (C) The city mayor
   (D) The company president

96. Look at the graphic. Which building will be affected by the first road closure?

   (A) The high school
   (B) The post office
   (C) The bus station
   (D) The museum

97. What information does the speaker say can be found on a Web site?

   (A) The location of a bus stop
   (B) The schedule for a construction project
   (C) Information about job openings
   (D) Steps for filing a complaint

98. According to the speaker, why should listeners visit the customer service desk?

   (A) To claim a lost item
   (B) To check extra baggage
   (C) To request a special meal
   (D) To volunteer for a later flight

99. Look at the graphic. Which information has changed?

   (A) Los Angeles
   (B) B1205
   (C) 22C
   (D) 8D

100. According to the speaker, what is the reason for the change?

   (A) Some workers are late.
   (B) A door is broken.
   (C) The weather is bad.
   (D) A computer is malfunctioning.

This is the end of the Listening test.

토익® 정기시험
기출문제집

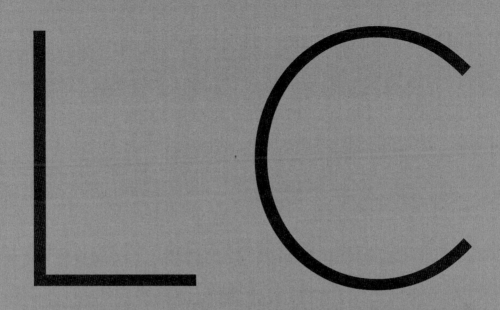

LC

기출 TEST

06

LISTENING TEST

In the Listening test, you will be asked to demonstrate how well you understand spoken English. The entire Listening test will last approximately 45 minutes. There are four parts, and directions are given for each part. You must mark your answers on the separate answer sheet. Do not write your answers in your test book.

PART 1

Directions: For each question in this part, you will hear four statements about a picture in your test book. When you hear the statements, you must select the one statement that best describes what you see in the picture. Then find the number of the question on your answer sheet and mark your answer. The statements will not be printed in your test book and will be spoken only one time.

Statement (C), "They're sitting at a table," is the best description of the picture, so you should select answer (C) and mark it on your answer sheet.

1.

2.

GO ON TO THE NEXT PAGE ➤

3.

4.

5.

6.

GO ON TO THE NEXT PAGE ➡

PART 2

Directions: You will hear a question or statement and three responses spoken in English. They will not be printed in your test book and will be spoken only one time. Select the best response to the question or statement and mark the letter (A), (B), or (C) on your answer sheet.

7. Mark your answer on your answer sheet.

8. Mark your answer on your answer sheet.

9. Mark your answer on your answer sheet.

10. Mark your answer on your answer sheet.

11. Mark your answer on your answer sheet.

12. Mark your answer on your answer sheet.

13. Mark your answer on your answer sheet.

14. Mark your answer on your answer sheet.

15. Mark your answer on your answer sheet.

16. Mark your answer on your answer sheet.

17. Mark your answer on your answer sheet.

18. Mark your answer on your answer sheet.

19. Mark your answer on your answer sheet.

20. Mark your answer on your answer sheet.

21. Mark your answer on your answer sheet.

22. Mark your answer on your answer sheet.

23. Mark your answer on your answer sheet.

24. Mark your answer on your answer sheet.

25. Mark your answer on your answer sheet.

26. Mark your answer on your answer sheet.

27. Mark your answer on your answer sheet.

28. Mark your answer on your answer sheet.

29. Mark your answer on your answer sheet.

30. Mark your answer on your answer sheet.

31. Mark your answer on your answer sheet.

PART 3

Directions: You will hear some conversations between two or more people. You will be asked to answer three questions about what the speakers say in each conversation. Select the best response to each question and mark the letter (A), (B), (C), or (D) on your answer sheet. The conversations will not be printed in your test book and will be spoken only one time.

32. Where do the speakers most likely work?

(A) At a movie theater
(B) At a construction firm
(C) At an art gallery
(D) At a furniture store

33. What problem are the speakers discussing?

(A) A display area is not clean.
(B) An appliance is broken.
(C) Some bills are not paid.
(D) Some materials are missing.

34. What will the man most likely do next?

(A) Request a recommendation
(B) Reserve a rental car
(C) Look for some replacement parts
(D) Contact some local companies

35. Why does the woman say she is visiting the city?

(A) To see a museum exhibit
(B) To attend a conference
(C) To receive an award
(D) To look at some real estate

36. What does the woman say she is concerned about?

(A) Being unable to get a ticket
(B) Booking a hotel room
(C) Having a wrong address
(D) Arriving late for an event

37. What does the man recommend doing?

(A) Looking at a map
(B) Checking an online site
(C) Buying a weekly pass
(D) Calling a friend

38. Where does the woman work?

(A) At a hotel
(B) At a café
(C) At an airport
(D) At a car rental agency

39. What is the man's complaint?

(A) An Internet connection is slow.
(B) A garage does not have enough parking.
(C) There is a billing error on a receipt.
(D) There are too few choices on a menu.

40. What does the woman say will happen next week?

(A) A price will increase.
(B) A construction project will begin.
(C) A shipment will arrive.
(D) A celebration will take place.

41. Where most likely are the speakers?

(A) At a bookstore
(B) At an art supply store
(C) At a clothing retailer
(D) At a supermarket

42. Why is the woman unable to receive a refund?

(A) She purchased a discounted item.
(B) She has lost a receipt.
(C) A store has changed a policy.
(D) A product has been damaged.

43. What does the man suggest?

(A) Exchanging an item
(B) Speaking with a manager
(C) Returning at a later time
(D) Applying for a rewards program

GO ON TO THE NEXT PAGE

44. What plan is the company considering?

    (A) Expanding its inventory
    (B) Updating its filing system
    (C) Hiring a new marketing director
    (D) Opening another location

45. What does the man imply when he says, "the marketing team has done the research"?

    (A) He is happy to not be assigned a task.
    (B) He disagrees with a colleague.
    (C) He does not want to hire more staff members.
    (D) He hopes an advertising campaign will begin soon.

46. What will take place in January?

    (A) A job interview
    (B) A board of directors meeting
    (C) A storewide sale
    (D) A focus group test

47. What department does the man work in?

    (A) Product Development
    (B) Maintenance
    (C) Human Resources
    (D) Accounting

48. What problem does the woman mention?

    (A) A password does not work.
    (B) A calculation was incorrect.
    (C) Some equipment is broken.
    (D) Some interns are unavailable.

49. What will the man most likely do next?

    (A) Speak with a supplier
    (B) Revise a document
    (C) Prepare an invoice
    (D) Call an assistant

50. Why did Mary miss her appointment?

    (A) Her meeting ran late.
    (B) Her bus was delayed.
    (C) She misread her calendar.
    (D) She overslept.

51. What is mentioned about Dr. García?

    (A) He recently won an award.
    (B) He is traveling for his job.
    (C) He writes for a medical journal.
    (D) He is an experienced surgeon.

52. What will Dr. Watanabe do next?

    (A) Sign a contract
    (B) Write a prescription
    (C) Order some lab supplies
    (D) Read a patient file

53. What does the woman ask the man about?

    (A) Building a patio
    (B) Renovating a lobby
    (C) Installing a light fixture
    (D) Constructing a parking garage

54. Why does the man recommend delaying a project?

    (A) His company is very busy.
    (B) Materials could be damaged.
    (C) Equipment costs may decrease.
    (D) A building permit is needed.

55. What will the woman most likely do next?

    (A) Call another company
    (B) Consult with a manager
    (C) Read some online reviews
    (D) Send photographs

56. What are the speakers mainly discussing?

(A) Updating a Web site
(B) Upgrading some machinery
(C) Developing a new product
(D) Planning a sales display

57. What does B Thompson International do?

(A) Provide vendor references
(B) Analyze online advertisements
(C) Deliver packages
(D) Conduct market research

58. What will the speakers probably do next?

(A) Get a cost estimate
(B) Interview some job candidates
(C) Organize a team meeting
(D) Finalize some designs

59. Who will be visiting the company?

(A) An international client
(B) A building superintendent
(C) A local politician
(D) A news reporter

60. Why does the woman say, "I'm attending the all-day software training on Monday"?

(A) She needs help with a technical problem.
(B) She is concerned about an expense.
(C) She is unable to fulfill a request.
(D) She is excited about an opportunity.

61. According to the man, what does the company hope to do next year?

(A) Promote some employees
(B) Open another office
(C) Improve public relations
(D) Publish an updated handbook

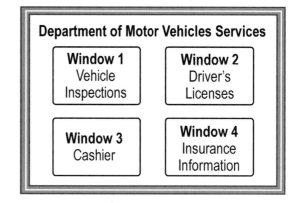

62. What is the man surprised about?

(A) The size of an office
(B) The length of a line
(C) A course requirement
(D) A registration fee

63. What does the man say he will do in July?

(A) Take a vacation
(B) Start a training course
(C) Buy a new car
(D) Move to another city

64. Look at the graphic. Which window does the woman send the man to?

(A) Window 1
(B) Window 2
(C) Window 3
(D) Window 4

TEST 6

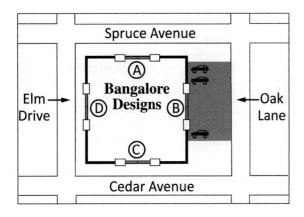

65. What does Bangalore Designs make?

(A) Household appliances
(B) Wooden furniture
(C) Construction equipment
(D) Paper products

66. Look at the graphic. Where will the man deliver some materials?

(A) At door A
(B) At door B
(C) At door C
(D) At door D

67. What will the woman do next?

(A) Go outside
(B) Send a text message
(C) Call a supervisor
(D) Prepare a payment

Vitamin A	Vitamin B6
watermelon	banana
Vitamin E	Vitamin C
papaya	orange

68. What do the speakers mainly discuss?

(A) Break-room renovations
(B) Updated cafeteria hours
(C) A healthy-eating program
(D) Results of an employee survey

69. Look at the graphic. Which fruit will the man most likely add to his diet?

(A) Watermelon
(B) Banana
(C) Orange
(D) Papaya

70. What does the man suggest doing?

(A) Ordering some lunch
(B) Providing feedback
(C) Attending a seminar
(D) Seeing a health-care provider

PART 4

Directions: You will hear some talks given by a single speaker. You will be asked to answer three questions about what the speaker says in each talk. Select the best response to each question and mark the letter (A), (B), (C), or (D) on your answer sheet. The talks will not be printed in your test book and will be spoken only one time.

71. Who most likely is the speaker?

(A) A software developer
(B) A magazine editor
(C) A hotel manager
(D) A travel agent

72. What is the talk mainly about?

(A) A travel itinerary
(B) A corporate merger
(C) Computer upgrades
(D) Work assignments

73. What does the speaker want the listeners to do tomorrow morning?

(A) Write some reports
(B) Buy airline tickets
(C) Fill out some time sheets
(D) Visit some local attractions

74. What kind of team does the speaker coach?

(A) Tennis
(B) Basketball
(C) Volleyball
(D) Badminton

75. What does the speaker say about his players?

(A) They practice every day.
(B) They will play in a competition.
(C) Most of them live far away.
(D) Many of them have jobs.

76. Why does the speaker say, "You've got the courts reserved from five to six"?

(A) To confirm an appointment
(B) To express surprise
(C) To request a change
(D) To congratulate a colleague

77. What does the speaker thank the listeners for?

(A) Making donations
(B) Packing some boxes
(C) Looking for some missing files
(D) Providing some suggestions

78. What is the speaker looking forward to?

(A) A sports activity
(B) A special performance
(C) A dinner
(D) A holiday

79. What will happen this afternoon?

(A) A client will visit.
(B) An office will close early.
(C) A construction project will end.
(D) A contract will be signed.

80. What does GS Incorporated manufacture?

(A) Commercial vehicles
(B) Cleaning supplies
(C) Fashion accessories
(D) Electronic devices

81. What has GS Incorporated recently started to do?

(A) Use environmentally friendly packaging
(B) Sell some products internationally
(C) Collaborate with another company
(D) Donate to charitable organizations

82. What will the listeners hear after the commercial break?

(A) A song
(B) A weather forecast
(C) An interview
(D) A traffic update

GO ON TO THE NEXT PAGE

83. What is the main topic of the broadcast?

    (A) Eating habits
    (B) Stress management
    (C) Exercise routines
    (D) Sleep issues

84. Why does the speaker say, "That's not a lot of time"?

    (A) To express concern about a deadline
    (B) To complain that a broadcast is too short
    (C) To emphasize the benefit of a program
    (D) To compliment some coworkers

85. According to the speaker, what should the listeners do first?

    (A) Ask a friend for help
    (B) Make a list of goals
    (C) Create a timeline
    (D) Purchase a handbook

86. What will happen at the Newport Museum on Saturday?

    (A) A parking area will be unavailable.
    (B) An award will be presented.
    (C) A gift shop will give discounts.
    (D) An interactive exhibit will open.

87. What does the speaker say about some Newport University students?

    (A) They raised money for some equipment.
    (B) They published a research paper.
    (C) They will give demonstrations at the museum.
    (D) They should submit job applications to the museum.

88. According to the speaker, what should the listeners do in advance?

    (A) Read about robots
    (B) Download a mobile app
    (C) Register for a class
    (D) Buy tickets

89. Why does the speaker say, "most of our sales team is new"?

    (A) To make a complaint
    (B) To decline a request
    (C) To extend an invitation
    (D) To give an explanation

90. What does the speaker show the listeners?

    (A) A company vacation policy
    (B) A sample time sheet
    (C) A list of organizations
    (D) A flow chart

91. What are the listeners expected to do by Friday?

    (A) Look at Internet sites
    (B) Obtain an identification badge
    (C) Provide an estimate
    (D) Respond to some questions

92. Why is the speaker calling?

    (A) To set up an interview
    (B) To finalize travel arrangements
    (C) To offer employment
    (D) To discuss an upcoming workshop

93. What does the speaker say the listener will be required to do?

    (A) Apply for a passport
    (B) Revise a document
    (C) Provide letters of recommendation
    (D) Move to another city

94. What does the speaker say will happen next week?

    (A) His company will be closed.
    (B) A holiday party will be held.
    (C) Registration will begin.
    (D) Some prices will be lowered.

Neighborhood Map

Interview Schedule for May 16	
Time	Candidate
10:00 A.M.	Bob Heilig
11:00 A.M.	Jihoon Lee
12:00 Noon	Susan Petersen
1:00 P.M.	Maya Gomez

95. What type of business does the speaker own?

(A) A taxi service
(B) A local grocery store
(C) A chain of restaurants
(D) A flower shop

96. Look at the graphic. In which neighborhood does the speaker want to offer a new service?

(A) Newbury
(B) Uptown
(C) Downtown
(D) Easton

97. What does the speaker want to discuss next?

(A) Advertising strategies
(B) Hiring procedures
(C) An updated vacation policy
(D) A renovation project

98. Why is the speaker unable to participate in one of the interviews?

(A) She is leaving for a business trip.
(B) She has a medical appointment.
(C) She is stuck in traffic.
(D) She has to finish an urgent assignment.

99. Look at the graphic. Who is the listener asked to interview?

(A) Bob Heilig
(B) Jihoon Lee
(C) Susan Petersen
(D) Maya Gomez

100. What does the speaker say she will do?

(A) Set up a training schedule
(B) Organize a teleconference
(C) Revise a job description
(D) E-mail some materials

This is the end of the Listening test.

TEST 6

토익® 정기시험
기출문제집

LC

기출 TEST

07

LISTENING TEST

In the Listening test, you will be asked to demonstrate how well you understand spoken English. The entire Listening test will last approximately 45 minutes. There are four parts, and directions are given for each part. You must mark your answers on the separate answer sheet. Do not write your answers in your test book.

PART 1

Directions: For each question in this part, you will hear four statements about a picture in your test book. When you hear the statements, you must select the one statement that best describes what you see in the picture. Then find the number of the question on your answer sheet and mark your answer. The statements will not be printed in your test book and will be spoken only one time.

Statement (C), "They're sitting at a table," is the best description of the picture, so you should select answer (C) and mark it on your answer sheet.

1.

2.

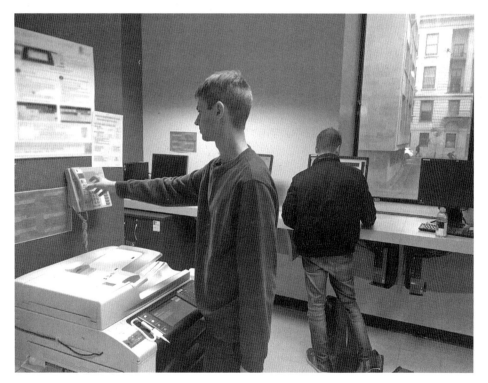

GO ON TO THE NEXT PAGE

3.

4.

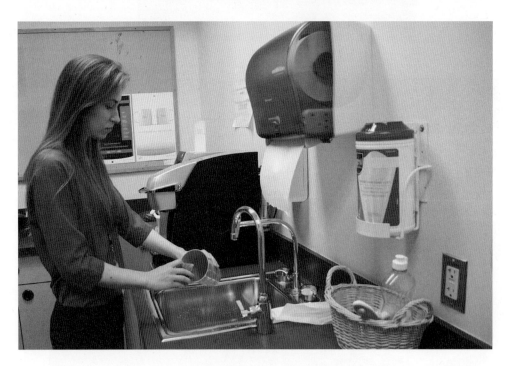

5.

6.

GO ON TO THE NEXT PAGE ➡

PART 2

Directions: You will hear a question or statement and three responses spoken in English. They will not be printed in your test book and will be spoken only one time. Select the best response to the question or statement and mark the letter (A), (B), or (C) on your answer sheet.

7. Mark your answer on your answer sheet.

8. Mark your answer on your answer sheet.

9. Mark your answer on your answer sheet.

10. Mark your answer on your answer sheet.

11. Mark your answer on your answer sheet.

12. Mark your answer on your answer sheet.

13. Mark your answer on your answer sheet.

14. Mark your answer on your answer sheet.

15. Mark your answer on your answer sheet.

16. Mark your answer on your answer sheet.

17. Mark your answer on your answer sheet.

18. Mark your answer on your answer sheet.

19. Mark your answer on your answer sheet.

20. Mark your answer on your answer sheet.

21. Mark your answer on your answer sheet.

22. Mark your answer on your answer sheet.

23. Mark your answer on your answer sheet.

24. Mark your answer on your answer sheet.

25. Mark your answer on your answer sheet.

26. Mark your answer on your answer sheet.

27. Mark your answer on your answer sheet.

28. Mark your answer on your answer sheet.

29. Mark your answer on your answer sheet.

30. Mark your answer on your answer sheet.

31. Mark your answer on your answer sheet.

PART 3

Directions: You will hear some conversations between two or more people. You will be asked to answer three questions about what the speakers say in each conversation. Select the best response to each question and mark the letter (A), (B), (C), or (D) on your answer sheet. The conversations will not be printed in your test book and will be spoken only one time.

32. Where does the conversation most likely take place?

(A) At a library
(B) At a theater
(C) At a museum
(D) At a restaurant

33. What problem does the man mention?

(A) A brochure contains an error.
(B) A shipment is late.
(C) A guest list has been misplaced.
(D) A computer is not working.

34. What will the woman most likely do next?

(A) Contact a coordinator
(B) Submit a work order
(C) Upload some images
(D) Purchase some supplies

35. Who most likely are the speakers?

(A) Cleaners
(B) Servers
(C) Nutritionists
(D) Food critics

36. Why will the man talk to some cooks?

(A) To compliment their work
(B) To ask for some advice
(C) To change an assignment
(D) To update an order

37. What does the man mean when he says, "I have tickets to a baseball game on Thursday"?

(A) He cannot help the woman.
(B) He has similar interests as the woman.
(C) He wants to invite the woman to an event.
(D) He is concerned that tickets will sell out.

38. Why is the man calling?

(A) To inquire about a job
(B) To request a prescription
(C) To ask about business hours
(D) To reschedule an appointment

39. What does the woman say about Dr. Ramirez?

(A) She is presenting at a conference next week.
(B) She works at two different locations.
(C) She teaches at a medical school.
(D) She usually does not work on Wednesdays.

40. What does the woman give to the man?

(A) Directions to a medical center
(B) A Web site address
(C) A phone number
(D) A cost estimate

41. Where are the speakers?

(A) At a supermarket
(B) At a furniture store
(C) At a clothing retailer
(D) At an automobile repair shop

42. Why does Tom ask the woman for help?

(A) A receipt is missing.
(B) A computer is broken.
(C) A warranty is expired.
(D) An item is out of stock.

43. What does the woman offer to do for the customer?

(A) Give him in-store credit
(B) Check a storage room
(C) Call another store
(D) Provide express delivery service

GO ON TO THE NEXT PAGE

44. What will take place this year?

(A) A corporate merger
(B) A software update
(C) A research study
(D) An office relocation

45. What problem does the man mention?

(A) Some paperwork has been lost.
(B) Some equipment is broken.
(C) Some funding was not approved.
(D) Some designs were rejected.

46. What will the woman do next?

(A) Revise a budget
(B) Schedule a meeting
(C) Find some contact information
(D) Hire a consultant

47. Where does the woman want to work?

(A) At a factory
(B) At a restaurant
(C) At a fitness center
(D) At a clothing store

48. Why did the woman leave her previous job?

(A) She began university studies.
(B) Her commute was too long.
(C) The company closed.
(D) The pay was low.

49. What does the man explain to the woman?

(A) There are evening shifts.
(B) A uniform will be provided.
(C) Training will be necessary.
(D) The company is very small.

50. Where are the speakers?

(A) At a pharmacy
(B) At a clothing store
(C) At a dental clinic
(D) At a fitness center

51. What does the woman explain to the man?

(A) He has missed an appointment.
(B) A price has changed.
(C) A business is closing soon.
(D) An item is not available.

52. What does the man say he will do?

(A) Complete a customer survey
(B) Return another day
(C) Look up some data
(D) Pay with a credit card

53. What does the woman ask the man to do?

(A) Review an order
(B) Set up a computer
(C) Organize a conference
(D) Contact a client

54. What will the man bring to the woman?

(A) A catalog
(B) A calendar
(C) A list of suppliers
(D) A building directory

55. What does the woman plan to do next week?

(A) Send out a newsletter
(B) Sign a contract
(C) Go on a trip
(D) Submit some slides

56. What are the speakers mainly discussing?

(A) A focus group
(B) Computer-use policies
(C) An upcoming merger
(D) Employee rewards

57. What does the man imply when he says, "You spend more time with your team than I do"?

(A) The woman's team requires more staff.
(B) The woman should schedule fewer meetings.
(C) The woman is the best person to decide.
(D) The woman should have noticed a mistake.

58. What does the man advise the woman to do next?

(A) Speak with a colleague
(B) Research a competitor
(C) Download an application
(D) Attend a seminar

59. What field do the speakers most likely work in?

(A) Engineering
(B) Accounting
(C) Education
(D) Advertising

60. What problem is mentioned?

(A) A power cord is missing.
(B) A microphone is not functioning properly.
(C) A screen is not displaying an image.
(D) A battery is not charging.

61. What does the woman suggest doing?

(A) Using a different computer
(B) Moving to another room
(C) Postponing a demonstration
(D) Contacting technical support

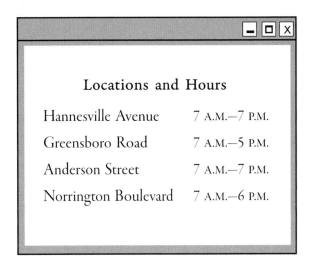

Locations and Hours

Hannesville Avenue	7 A.M.–7 P.M.
Greensboro Road	7 A.M.–5 P.M.
Anderson Street	7 A.M.–7 P.M.
Norrington Boulevard	7 A.M.–6 P.M.

62. Where does the man work?

(A) At a furniture store
(B) At a painting company
(C) At a bakery
(D) At a gym

63. What does the woman say is important?

(A) A healthy option
(B) A low price
(C) A fast delivery
(D) A specific decoration

64. Look at the graphic. Which location did the woman call?

(A) Hannesville Avenue
(B) Greensboro Road
(C) Anderson Street
(D) Norrington Boulevard

TEST 7

GO ON TO THE NEXT PAGE

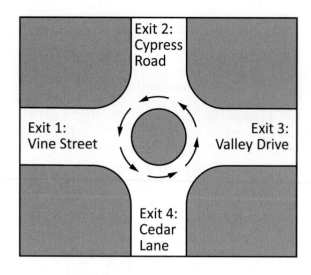

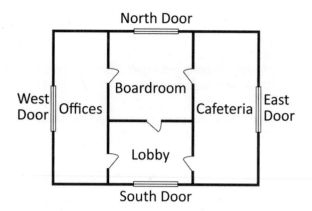

65. What event are the speakers going to attend?

    (A) A concert
    (B) A marathon
    (C) An art show
    (D) A restaurant festival

66. Who most likely are the speakers?

    (A) Chefs
    (B) Musicians
    (C) Investors
    (D) Journalists

67. Look at the graphic. Which road will the speakers take next?

    (A) Vine Street
    (B) Cypress Road
    (C) Valley Drive
    (D) Cedar Lane

68. What most likely is the woman's job title?

    (A) Custodian
    (B) Locksmith
    (C) Landscaper
    (D) Parking attendant

69. Look at the graphic. Which door are the speakers discussing?

    (A) The North Door
    (B) The East Door
    (C) The South Door
    (D) The West Door

70. What does the man remind the woman to do?

    (A) Display her badge
    (B) Store her belongings
    (C) Submit her time sheet
    (D) Validate her parking pass

PART 4

Directions: You will hear some talks given by a single speaker. You will be asked to answer three questions about what the speaker says in each talk. Select the best response to each question and mark the letter (A), (B), (C), or (D) on your answer sheet. The talks will not be printed in your test book and will be spoken only one time.

71. What is the news report mainly about?

(A) A museum exhibit
(B) A holiday parade
(C) A building renovation
(D) A sports competition

72. Who is Byron Lang?

(A) A travel agent
(B) An architect
(C) A city official
(D) An athlete

73. What does the speaker say will be provided next year?

(A) Extra parking
(B) Weekend tours
(C) Souvenirs
(D) Job opportunities

74. What will be installed this weekend?

(A) Drinking fountains
(B) Videoconferencing equipment
(C) An air-conditioning system
(D) An alarm system

75. According to the speaker, why is the change being made?

(A) To reduce costs
(B) To increase comfort
(C) To boost productivity
(D) To comply with guidelines

76. What should the listeners do before they leave work on Friday?

(A) Talk to their managers
(B) Move their cars
(C) Cover their desks
(D) Complete a questionnaire

77. Why has the speaker arranged the meeting?

(A) To go over sales data
(B) To distribute client information
(C) To give a demonstration
(D) To assign special projects

78. What should the listeners assure clients about?

(A) Orders will be processed on time.
(B) Contracts will be mailed.
(C) Discounts will be applied.
(D) Factory tours will be available.

79. What does the speaker imply when she says, "I had to read through the manual twice"?

(A) A company policy is surprising.
(B) A publication may contain some errors.
(C) A manual was updated.
(D) A software program may be difficult to learn.

80. What type of business created the tutorial?

(A) A post office
(B) A community college
(C) An electronics company
(D) A paper goods manufacturer

81. According to the speaker, what should the listeners print out?

(A) A shipping label
(B) A manual
(C) An invoice
(D) Installation directions

82. What does the speaker offer to the listeners?

(A) A warranty
(B) A discount
(C) Free accessories
(D) Express delivery

GO ON TO THE NEXT PAGE

83. What has the company decided to do?

(A) Launch a Web site
(B) Create a new type of beverage
(C) Sell products in vending machines
(D) Advertise in sports magazines

84. What did a survey indicate about customers?

(A) They prefer natural ingredients.
(B) They make online purchases.
(C) They like celebrity promotions.
(D) They want lower prices.

85. What are the listeners asked to do?

(A) Try a sample
(B) Review a proposal
(C) Submit suggestions
(D) Contact some customers

86. What type of business does the speaker work in?

(A) Automobile sales
(B) Interior design
(C) Food distribution
(D) Paper manufacturing

87. According to the survey results, what do customers like about the speaker's company?

(A) The quality of its products
(B) The location of its branches
(C) Its dedication to customer satisfaction
(D) Its innovative advertisements

88. What does the speaker imply when he says, "You're familiar with Fox International Deliveries, aren't you"?

(A) He wants to change service providers.
(B) He wants the listener to give a presentation.
(C) He wants to promote the listener to a new role.
(D) He wants to merge with another company.

89. What is the speaker shopping for?

(A) Groceries
(B) Kitchen appliances
(C) Sporting goods
(D) Computer accessories

90. What does the speaker mean when he says, "it's pretty far from here"?

(A) He is unable to complete a task today.
(B) He will need to borrow a car.
(C) He may be late for an appointment.
(D) He needs driving directions.

91. What does the speaker ask the listener to do?

(A) Print a document
(B) Address some letters
(C) Arrange an interview
(D) Process a refund

92. What industry does the speaker work in?

(A) Electronics
(B) Finance
(C) Marketing
(D) Tourism

93. How does the speaker say she stays informed about current trends?

(A) She follows social networking sites.
(B) She analyzes consumer reviews.
(C) She reads industry journals.
(D) She interviews movie stars.

94. What does the speaker suggest changing?

(A) Where to open a new office
(B) When to sell certain products
(C) How to arrange a display
(D) What brands to carry

LEBBINSVILLE AMUSEMENT PARK
Grand Opening: August 12

Special Events All Summer!

Wednesdays	Comedy Special
Thursdays	Magic Show
Fridays	Music Performance
Saturdays	Parade

	Mon.	Tues.	Wed.	Thurs.
8:00	Planning meeting			
9:00		Work on budget report	Leadership training	Finish budget report
10:00	Presentation		Directors' strategy meeting	
1:00		Team meeting		

95. Who most likely is the speaker?

(A) A park owner
(B) A journalist
(C) An electrician
(D) A graphic designer

96. Look at the graphic. Which special event was canceled?

(A) The Comedy Special
(B) The Magic Show
(C) The Music Performance
(D) The Parade

97. What will the speaker do this afternoon?

(A) Introduce a guest
(B) Show a video
(C) Describe a contest
(D) Make a phone call

98. What is the speaker concerned about?

(A) A short timeline
(B) An advertising campaign
(C) Technical issues
(D) Inexperienced staff

99. Look at the graphic. When does the speaker suggest meeting?

(A) On Monday
(B) On Tuesday
(C) On Wednesday
(D) On Thursday

100. What does the speaker ask the listener to do?

(A) Finalize a construction schedule
(B) Review a budget
(C) Create a meeting agenda
(D) Call a potential client

TEST 7

This is the end of the Listening test.

토익 정기시험
기출문제집

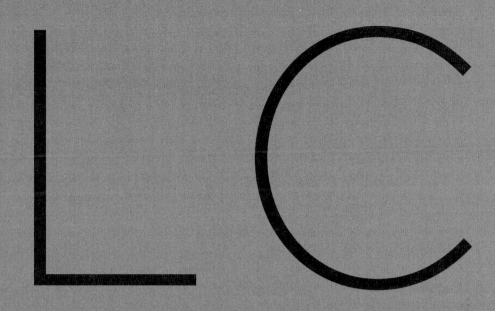

LC

ETS TEST

08

LISTENING TEST

In the Listening test, you will be asked to demonstrate how well you understand spoken English. The entire Listening test will last approximately 45 minutes. There are four parts, and directions are given for each part. You must mark your answers on the separate answer sheet. Do not write your answers in your test book.

PART 1

Directions: For each question in this part, you will hear four statements about a picture in your test book. When you hear the statements, you must select the one statement that best describes what you see in the picture. Then find the number of the question on your answer sheet and mark your answer. The statements will not be printed in your test book and will be spoken only one time.

Statement (C), "They're sitting at a table," is the best description of the picture, so you should select answer (C) and mark it on your answer sheet.

1.

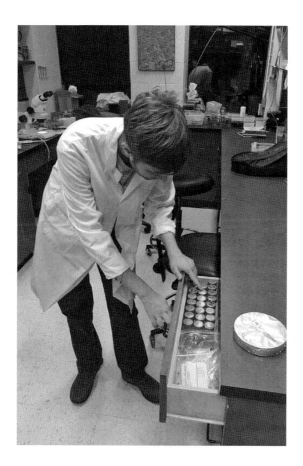

2.

GO ON TO THE NEXT PAGE

3.

4.

5.

6.

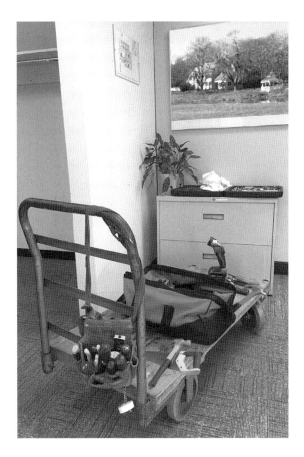

GO ON TO THE NEXT PAGE ➡

PART 2

Directions: You will hear a question or statement and three responses spoken in English. They will not be printed in your test book and will be spoken only one time. Select the best response to the question or statement and mark the letter (A), (B), or (C) on your answer sheet.

7. Mark your answer on your answer sheet.

8. Mark your answer on your answer sheet.

9. Mark your answer on your answer sheet.

10. Mark your answer on your answer sheet.

11. Mark your answer on your answer sheet.

12. Mark your answer on your answer sheet.

13. Mark your answer on your answer sheet.

14. Mark your answer on your answer sheet.

15. Mark your answer on your answer sheet.

16. Mark your answer on your answer sheet.

17. Mark your answer on your answer sheet.

18. Mark your answer on your answer sheet.

19. Mark your answer on your answer sheet.

20. Mark your answer on your answer sheet.

21. Mark your answer on your answer sheet.

22. Mark your answer on your answer sheet.

23. Mark your answer on your answer sheet.

24. Mark your answer on your answer sheet.

25. Mark your answer on your answer sheet.

26. Mark your answer on your answer sheet.

27. Mark your answer on your answer sheet.

28. Mark your answer on your answer sheet.

29. Mark your answer on your answer sheet.

30. Mark your answer on your answer sheet.

31. Mark your answer on your answer sheet.

Directions: You will hear some conversations between two or more people. You will be asked to answer three questions about what the speakers say in each conversation. Select the best response to each question and mark the letter (A), (B), (C), or (D) on your answer sheet. The conversations will not be printed in your test book and will be spoken only one time.

32. What did the woman purchase?

    (A) A piano
    (B) A refrigerator
    (C) Some windows
    (D) Some gardening tools

33. Why does the man apologize?

    (A) He lost the woman's phone number.
    (B) A coupon has expired.
    (C) An item is out of stock.
    (D) A delivery is delayed.

34. What does the woman say she will do tomorrow morning?

    (A) Mail a contract
    (B) Tour a model home
    (C) Leave for vacation
    (D) Look at samples

35. What are the speakers preparing for?

    (A) A training session
    (B) A board meeting
    (C) A press conference
    (D) A product demonstration

36. What problem does the woman mention?

    (A) Some presenters will be late.
    (B) Some equipment is not working.
    (C) An event schedule is incorrect.
    (D) A meeting room is too small.

37. What does the man say he will do?

    (A) E-mail a coworker
    (B) Hang up some posters
    (C) Make an announcement
    (D) Copy some documents

38. Where do the women work?

    (A) At an advertising firm
    (B) At a music studio
    (C) At a manufacturing plant
    (D) At a department store

39. What does the man say about a product?

    (A) It comes in many colors.
    (B) It has a warranty.
    (C) It is made of quality materials.
    (D) It is only available online.

40. What does Helen recommend doing?

    (A) Increasing a budget
    (B) Developing a timeline
    (C) Checking some customer reviews
    (D) Contacting some local suppliers

41. What kind of class is the woman interested in?

    (A) Dance
    (B) Strength training
    (C) Swimming
    (D) Yoga

42. What does the man suggest the woman do?

    (A) Invite a friend to join her
    (B) Try a free class
    (C) Return at a later time
    (D) Sign up for a membership

43. What special offer does the woman qualify for?

    (A) A guest pass
    (B) A student discount
    (C) A private lesson
    (D) A free water bottle

TEST 8

GO ON TO THE NEXT PAGE

44. Where does the man work?

   (A) At a hotel
   (B) At a department store
   (C) At a dentist's office
   (D) At a bank

45. What does the woman say about a form?

   (A) She would like her own copy.
   (B) She would prefer to access it online.
   (C) She needs it to be translated.
   (D) She has already completed one.

46. What will the woman do this afternoon?

   (A) Register for a workshop
   (B) Meet a client for lunch
   (C) Train some employees
   (D) Tour a facility

---

47. Who most likely is the woman?

   (A) An architect
   (B) An interior decorator
   (C) A property manager
   (D) A city official

48. What are the men concerned about?

   (A) The number of meeting rooms
   (B) The amount of storage space
   (C) The date of a deadline
   (D) The size of a budget

49. What benefit does the woman mention?

   (A) Delivery service is available.
   (B) Transportation is inexpensive.
   (C) A building is in the city center.
   (D) A parking area is nearby.

---

50. What type of business do the speakers work for?

   (A) A fashion magazine
   (B) A clothing manufacturer
   (C) An employment agency
   (D) An advertising agency

51. What does the man suggest doing?

   (A) Modifying a blueprint
   (B) Opening a retail location
   (C) Purchasing new equipment
   (D) Hiring additional staff

52. What does the woman say she will do?

   (A) Read some e-mails
   (B) Contact a supervisor
   (C) Work overtime
   (D) Increase prices

---

53. Why is the man calling?

   (A) To complain about a delay
   (B) To interview for a job
   (C) To ask about a company program
   (D) To confirm a management decision

54. What does the man imply when he says, "I'm supposed to start my shift at noon"?

   (A) He cannot attend an event.
   (B) He wants to end a conversation.
   (C) He needs some supplies immediately.
   (D) He was given the wrong assignment.

55. What does the man say about a company's Web site?

   (A) It is under construction.
   (B) It has a useful map.
   (C) A password is required to view it.
   (D) Some information on it is unclear.

---

56. Who most likely is the woman?

(A) A writer
(B) A musician
(C) A television show host
(D) A photographer

57. What does the man encourage the woman to do?

(A) Update some contact information
(B) Review a project proposal
(C) Submit an invoice
(D) Interview for a position

58. What topic does the woman say she is interested in?

(A) Landscape design
(B) Modern architecture
(C) Folk music
(D) Street artwork

---

59. What event is being discussed?

(A) A company picnic
(B) A professional conference
(C) A grand opening
(D) An investors meeting

60. What does the man imply when he says, "let me call his assistant"?

(A) He will volunteer to prepare a speech.
(B) He will find a new location.
(C) He will ask for a schedule change.
(D) He will make a complaint.

61. What does the woman say she will do?

(A) Print out a map
(B) Confirm a catering order
(C) Clean some sports equipment
(D) Mail some invitations

EXHIBITOR MAP

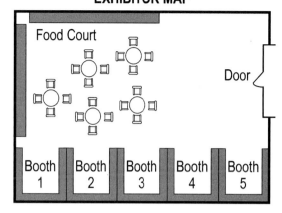

62. What business does the man most likely work in?

(A) Electronics
(B) Clothing
(C) Gardening
(D) Cookware

63. Look at the graphic. Which booth will the man be assigned to?

(A) Booth 1
(B) Booth 2
(C) Booth 4
(D) Booth 5

64. What does the woman say she will send to the man?

(A) Admission tickets
(B) An identification badge
(C) A registration receipt
(D) A parking permit

TEST 8

GO ON TO THE NEXT PAGE

Market Share

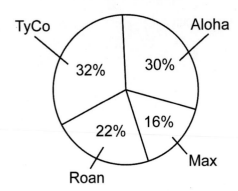

Interview schedule

Name	Time	Type of interview
Tim Bartlett	10:00	On-site
Brandy Miller	11:00	Videoconference
Louisa Sanchez	1:00	Videoconference
Ken Mori	2:00	On-site

65. What product are the speakers discussing?

(A) Kitchen appliances
(B) Children's shoes
(C) Photo editing software
(D) Gardening tools

66. Look at the graphic. Which brand does the woman mention?

(A) Aloha
(B) Max
(C) Roan
(D) TyCo

67. What will the woman go get from her office?

(A) Some samples
(B) Some data reports
(C) A key
(D) A résumé

68. What position is the company interviewing for?

(A) Accountant
(B) Graphic designer
(C) Computer programmer
(D) Screenwriter

69. What does the woman ask about?

(A) What the job requirements are
(B) How many people applied
(C) Whether references are necessary
(D) Whether some equipment is ready

70. Look at the graphic. Which candidate is overseas?

(A) Tim Bartlett
(B) Brandy Miller
(C) Louisa Sanchez
(D) Ken Mori

Directions: You will hear some talks given by a single speaker. You will be asked to answer three questions about what the speaker says in each talk. Select the best response to each question and mark the letter (A), (B), (C), or (D) on your answer sheet. The talks will not be printed in your test book and will be spoken only one time.

71. What type of product is the speaker mainly discussing?

   (A) Refrigerators
   (B) Laptops
   (C) Swimsuits
   (D) Teas

72. Why is the speaker pleased?

   (A) Packaging has been improved.
   (B) A deadline has been extended.
   (C) Sales have increased.
   (D) A budget was approved.

73. What would the speaker like to do?

   (A) Give the sales team a bonus
   (B) Purchase new equipment
   (C) Survey some consumers
   (D) Enter into a long-term contract

74. What does the speaker say are available by the door?

   (A) Flowers
   (B) Coupons
   (C) Umbrellas
   (D) Guidebooks

75. Why will the listeners visit a sculpture garden first?

   (A) It is nearby.
   (B) It closes soon.
   (C) It is hosting an activity.
   (D) It is a popular attraction.

76. Why does the speaker say, "I'll be eating at the Spruce Road Café"?

   (A) To make a recommendation
   (B) To volunteer for a task
   (C) To ask for directions
   (D) To explain a delay

77. What is the advertisement about?

   (A) An art exhibition
   (B) A Web site builder
   (C) A smartphone
   (D) A print shop

78. According to the speaker, why will the listeners be surprised?

   (A) Shipping is free.
   (B) Staff members are certified.
   (C) A location is convenient.
   (D) A product is easy to use.

79. What does the speaker encourage the listeners to do?

   (A) Attend an event
   (B) Sign up for a trial
   (C) Make a phone call
   (D) Read customer reviews

80. Where will the speaker go next Tuesday?

   (A) To a store
   (B) To a factory
   (C) To a hotel
   (D) To an airport

81. Why will the speaker bring his laptop?

   (A) To try out some new software
   (B) To fix a technical problem
   (C) To conduct a video conference
   (D) To check competitors' prices

82. What does the speaker mean when he says, "I don't think the traffic will be that bad"?

   (A) He plans to drive.
   (B) He expects to arrive early.
   (C) He does not need a map.
   (D) He wants to postpone a departure time.

GO ON TO THE NEXT PAGE

TEST 8

83. What is Soonja Lee's profession?

(A) Doctor
(B) Chef
(C) Farmer
(D) Teacher

84. According to the speaker, what does Soonja Lee emphasize?

(A) Eating healthy foods
(B) Practicing cooking skills
(C) Shopping locally
(D) Taking courses

85. Why should the listeners stay after the speech?

(A) To ask questions
(B) To enter a contest
(C) To see a demonstration
(D) To buy a book

86. What is the main topic of the talk?

(A) A vacation policy
(B) A new project
(C) A revised budget
(D) Some customer complaints

87. Why does the speaker say, "we'll be hiring a new programmer to provide support"?

(A) To reassure the listeners regarding a timeline
(B) To encourage the listeners to apply for a position
(C) To respond to customer feedback
(D) To suggest that more office space is needed

88. What does the speaker ask the listeners to do?

(A) Change their passwords
(B) Call Human Resources
(C) Talk with Technical Support
(D) Update a calendar

89. Where does the speaker most likely work?

(A) At a construction site
(B) At a manufacturing plant
(C) At a landscaping company
(D) At a public transportation office

90. What are the listeners instructed to wear?

(A) Helmets
(B) Uniforms
(C) Safety glasses
(D) Ear protection

91. According to the speaker, what will the listeners do at ten o'clock?

(A) Have a meal
(B) Conduct an inspection
(C) Attend a workshop
(D) Meet a supervisor

92. What type of business is the broadcast about?

(A) An energy company
(B) A real estate firm
(C) A travel agency
(D) A film studio

93. What will the business offer every Saturday?

(A) Trip discounts
(B) Free consultations
(C) Training sessions
(D) Facility tours

94. According to the speaker, what can the listeners do at a library?

(A) Register for an event
(B) Pick up a map
(C) Hear a talk
(D) Board a shuttle bus

Departs	Day	Price
9:00 A.M.	Thursday, June 16	$280
6:00 P.M.	Friday, June 17	$375
8:00 A.M.	Saturday, June 18	$310
3:00 P.M.	Sunday, June 19	$345

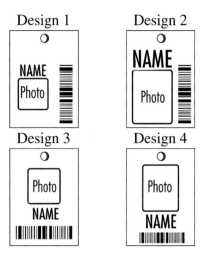

Design 1 Design 2

Design 3 Design 4

95. Why does the speaker have to delay a trip?

(A) She has to renew her passport.
(B) She wants to avoid bad weather.
(C) She has to attend a work event.
(D) She wants to get a cheaper ticket.

96. Look at the graphic. How much will the speaker pay for a flight?

(A) $280
(B) $375
(C) $310
(D) $345

97. What does the speaker ask the listener to do?

(A) Check a schedule
(B) Recommend a hotel
(C) Send some documents
(D) Rent a car

98. What has the speaker's company recently done?

(A) It increased building security.
(B) It started an internship program.
(C) It merged with another company.
(D) It introduced a new logo.

99. Look at the graphic. Which badge design did the speaker choose?

(A) Design 1
(B) Design 2
(C) Design 3
(D) Design 4

100. What should the listeners do by Friday?

(A) Have their photos taken
(B) Post their résumés
(C) Call a maintenance worker
(D) Submit a payment

This is the end of the Listening test.

TEST 8

토익® 정기시험
기출문제집

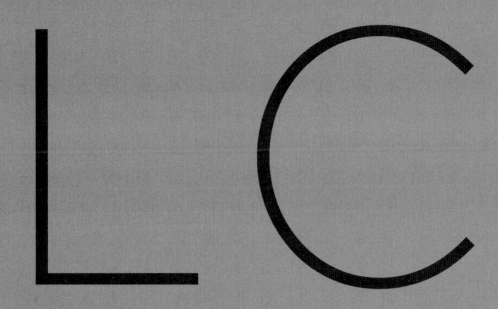

LC

ETS TEST

09

LISTENING TEST

In the Listening test, you will be asked to demonstrate how well you understand spoken English. The entire Listening test will last approximately 45 minutes. There are four parts, and directions are given for each part. You must mark your answers on the separate answer sheet. Do not write your answers in your test book.

PART 1

Directions: For each question in this part, you will hear four statements about a picture in your test book. When you hear the statements, you must select the one statement that best describes what you see in the picture. Then find the number of the question on your answer sheet and mark your answer. The statements will not be printed in your test book and will be spoken only one time.

Statement (C), "They're sitting at a table," is the best description of the picture, so you should select answer (C) and mark it on your answer sheet.

1.

2.

GO ON TO THE NEXT PAGE

TEST 9

3.

4.

5.

6.

GO ON TO THE NEXT PAGE

TEST 9

9

PART 2

Directions: You will hear a question or statement and three responses spoken in English. They will not be printed in your test book and will be spoken only one time. Select the best response to the question or statement and mark the letter (A), (B), or (C) on your answer sheet.

7. Mark your answer on your answer sheet.

8. Mark your answer on your answer sheet.

9. Mark your answer on your answer sheet.

10. Mark your answer on your answer sheet.

11. Mark your answer on your answer sheet.

12. Mark your answer on your answer sheet.

13. Mark your answer on your answer sheet.

14. Mark your answer on your answer sheet.

15. Mark your answer on your answer sheet.

16. Mark your answer on your answer sheet.

17. Mark your answer on your answer sheet.

18. Mark your answer on your answer sheet.

19. Mark your answer on your answer sheet.

20. Mark your answer on your answer sheet.

21. Mark your answer on your answer sheet.

22. Mark your answer on your answer sheet.

23. Mark your answer on your answer sheet.

24. Mark your answer on your answer sheet.

25. Mark your answer on your answer sheet.

26. Mark your answer on your answer sheet.

27. Mark your answer on your answer sheet.

28. Mark your answer on your answer sheet.

29. Mark your answer on your answer sheet.

30. Mark your answer on your answer sheet.

31. Mark your answer on your answer sheet.

Directions: You will hear some conversations between two or more people. You will be asked to answer three questions about what the speakers say in each conversation. Select the best response to each question and mark the letter (A), (B), (C), or (D) on your answer sheet. The conversations will not be printed in your test book and will be spoken only one time.

32. Where does the man work?

    (A) At a grocery store
    (B) At an office supply store
    (C) At a gift shop
    (D) At an advertising firm

33. Why does the woman call the business?

    (A) To ask about a product
    (B) To confirm a delivery
    (C) To praise an employee
    (D) To inquire about job openings

34. What does the man say he will do?

    (A) Provide a coupon
    (B) Update a Web site
    (C) Meet with a client
    (D) Speak to a manager

35. What does the woman ask about?

    (A) The time of an event
    (B) The name of a client
    (C) The location of a meeting
    (D) The cost of an order

36. What problem does the woman mention?

    (A) Some equipment is not working.
    (B) Some documents are missing.
    (C) An agenda is incorrect.
    (D) An employee is absent.

37. What does Steve ask for permission to do?

    (A) Revise a contract
    (B) Make some announcements
    (C) Complete a purchase
    (D) Leave work early

38. What did the woman recently do?

    (A) She moved to a new area.
    (B) She published a book.
    (C) She participated in a news conference.
    (D) She purchased a mobile phone.

39. What does the man say about Dr. Chan?

    (A) She is available on weekends.
    (B) She speaks several languages.
    (C) She conducts research.
    (D) She works for a university.

40. What does the man say he will do?

    (A) Arrange a client luncheon
    (B) Move some furniture
    (C) Give the woman a business card
    (D) Show the woman an informational video

41. What did the man do last week?

    (A) He conducted a safety inspection.
    (B) He competed in an athletic tournament.
    (C) He took a family vacation.
    (D) He led a city government meeting.

42. What are the speakers mainly talking about?

    (A) Methods of training employees
    (B) Methods of paying for parking
    (C) How to use protective equipment
    (D) How to choose an insurance policy

43. What will the man probably do next?

    (A) Charge a credit card
    (B) Approve a budget
    (C) Pick up a new uniform
    (D) Demonstrate a mobile application

TEST 9

GO ON TO THE NEXT PAGE

44. Who is Ken Jacobs?

(A) An architect
(B) A chef
(C) A furniture designer
(D) A theater owner

45. What priority does the woman mention?

(A) Using local products
(B) Reducing expenses
(C) Finding qualified employees
(D) Providing more seating

46. What will the speakers do next?

(A) Walk around a building
(B) Estimate some prices
(C) Look at some plans
(D) Discuss permit requirements

47. What product are the speakers discussing?

(A) An electric tool
(B) A light fixture
(C) A safety helmet
(D) A laptop computer

48. Why does the man say, "I have the warranty right here"?

(A) To indicate that he is confused
(B) To prove that he is correct
(C) To finalize a purchase
(D) To decline an offer

49. What does the man suggest the woman do?

(A) Have an item repaired
(B) Read a manual
(C) Take some photographs
(D) Complete a survey

50. Where do the speakers work?

(A) At a call center
(B) At a travel agency
(C) At a repair shop
(D) At a shipping facility

51. Why does the woman say, "Ten new customers is a lot"?

(A) To support a decision
(B) To praise a colleague
(C) To request a promotion
(D) To express concern

52. What does the man offer to do?

(A) Speak with a supervisor
(B) Provide some feedback
(C) Check some inventory
(D) Order some tools

53. What are the speakers discussing?

(A) A job transfer
(B) A trade show
(C) A market survey
(D) A new product

54. What did the man's team do to stay competitive?

(A) They worked more efficiently.
(B) They used inexpensive materials.
(C) They recruited top candidates.
(D) They offered discounts.

55. What will the woman do next?

(A) E-mail some managers
(B) Order some equipment
(C) Schedule a team meeting
(D) Confirm a reservation

56. What is the woman's job?

(A) Travel agent
(B) Pilot
(C) Journalist
(D) Lawyer

57. What did the woman do last week?

(A) She toured a facility.
(B) She received a business loan.
(C) She attended a trade show.
(D) She conducted job interviews.

58. What problem does the woman mention?

(A) A flight was canceled.
(B) An office was closed.
(C) Some signatures are missing.
(D) More photographs are needed.

59. What does the company want to do?

(A) Hold a focus group
(B) Expand into new markets
(C) Hire an architect
(D) Develop a new Web site

60. Why did the woman invite the man to the meeting?

(A) To present the results of data analysis
(B) To develop a slide show for clients
(C) To announce a new store location
(D) To prepare for a shareholders' meeting

61. What will the meeting attendees most likely do next?

(A) Report on individual progress
(B) Look at some design plans
(C) Discuss some marketing ideas
(D) Create a project timeline

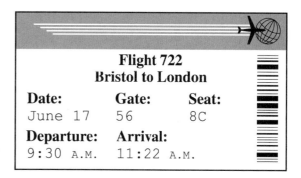

Flight 722		
Bristol to London		
Date:	**Gate:**	**Seat:**
June 17	56	8C
Departure:	**Arrival:**	
9:30 A.M.	11:22 A.M.	

62. Look at the graphic. What information has just changed?

(A) June 17
(B) 56
(C) 8C
(D) 9:30 A.M.

63. What has caused the change?

(A) A flight is overbooked.
(B) A computer is not working.
(C) Weather conditions are poor.
(D) A flight crew has arrived late.

64. What does the woman give to the man?

(A) A meal voucher
(B) A Web site address
(C) A password
(D) A receipt

GO ON TO THE NEXT PAGE

TEST 9

Rose Bloom Hotel, January 18

Maintenance Tasks	Location
Paint walls	Orchid Room
Repair the television	Room 156
Replace lightbulbs	Lilac Conference Room
Install new carpet	Room 444

Expenses

Equipment	$300	
Marketing	$520	
Utilities	$160	
Travel	$75	

65. Why does the woman apologize?

(A) She damaged an item.
(B) She arrived late to work.
(C) She missed a meeting.
(D) She forgot to file a report.

66. Look at the graphic. Which maintenance task is a priority?

(A) Painting walls
(B) Repairing the television
(C) Replacing lightbulbs
(D) Installing new carpet

67. What is the man looking for?

(A) A guest list
(B) A conference schedule
(C) Registration forms
(D) Maps of the area

68. What does the woman say she is pleased about?

(A) Employee performance
(B) Increased sales
(C) A positive review
(D) A store location

69. Look at the graphic. Which category amount needs to be updated?

(A) Equipment
(B) Marketing
(C) Utilities
(D) Travel

70. What does the man offer to do?

(A) Correct an online catalog
(B) Adjust a budget
(C) Consult another business owner
(D) Postpone a business trip

Directions: You will hear some talks given by a single speaker. You will bc asked to answer three questions about what the speaker says in each talk. Select the best response to each question and mark the letter (A), (B), (C), or (D) on your answer sheet. The talks will not be printed in your test book and will be spoken only one time.

71. What is the topic of the announcement?

(A) Healthy eating options
(B) Exercise sessions
(C) Professional-development courses
(D) Volunteer opportunities

72. What benefit does the speaker mention?

(A) Decreased expenses
(B) Personal satisfaction
(C) Increased productivity
(D) Improved qualifications

73. What should interested listeners do?

(A) Fill out a form
(B) Make a reservation
(C) Send a text message
(D) Get a supervisor's approval

74. What does the speaker say is unique about a restaurant?

(A) There is live music every night.
(B) Vegetables are grown locally.
(C) Food is prepared at the table.
(D) Customers can pay by mobile phone.

75. According to the speaker, what can the listeners do online?

(A) Check an event calendar
(B) Book a catering service
(C) Get directions to a location
(D) Download a coupon

76. What will begin next month?

(A) A customer loyalty program
(B) A cooking class
(C) A dining room renovation
(D) A hiring event

77. Where most likely are the listeners?

(A) At a board meeting
(B) At an airport
(C) At a television studio
(D) At a convention

78. What does the speaker mean when she says, "this will be your last stop"?

(A) The listeners will want to buy a product.
(B) An event is ending soon.
(C) An itinerary has changed.
(D) A company will no longer sell an item.

79. According to the speaker, what is unique about a product?

(A) The size
(B) The price
(C) The weight
(D) The color

80. What is the news report mainly about?

(A) A tourism initiative
(B) Plans for a city property
(C) The results of an election
(D) The price of housing

81. According to the speaker, why has the local population increased?

(A) A university has been built.
(B) Public transportation has improved.
(C) More jobs are available.
(D) Some historical sites have opened.

82. What does the speaker mean when he says, "they had the highest attendance there ever"?

(A) He has been a reporter for many years.
(B) Future meetings will need to be held somewhere else.
(C) Residents are very interested in a topic.
(D) The city hall has finally been renovated.

TEST 9

GO ON TO THE NEXT PAGE

83. Why is the speaker calling?

    (A) To make a payment
    (B) To request a refund
    (C) To ask about a return policy
    (D) To report a missing item

84. What does the speaker say she is preparing for?

    (A) A client meeting
    (B) A trade show
    (C) A job interview
    (D) A staff meeting

85. According to the speaker, what information was incorrect?

    (A) An invoice amount
    (B) A telephone number
    (C) A mailing address
    (D) A credit card number

86. Where does the speaker work?

    (A) At a university
    (B) At a library
    (C) At a publishing company
    (D) At an art gallery

87. What does the speaker say he would like to see?

    (A) An artist's biography
    (B) A calendar of events
    (C) Some blueprints
    (D) Some writing samples

88. According to the speaker, what is the problem with a construction project?

    (A) It blocks his view.
    (B) It is very noisy.
    (C) It has increased traffic.
    (D) It is over budget.

89. Why will a group from Korea visit the hotel next week?

    (A) To perform a safety inspection
    (B) To attend an industry conference
    (C) To research a magazine article
    (D) To discuss a possible investment

90. What does the speaker instruct Ms. Carlyle to do?

    (A) Find new suppliers
    (B) Arrange a dinner
    (C) Train some servers
    (D) Purchase new uniforms

91. Why does the speaker say, "I know Soo-Bin can speak Korean"?

    (A) To make a suggestion
    (B) To refuse an offer
    (C) To make an excuse
    (D) To correct a mistake

92. What is being advertised?

    (A) A delivery service
    (B) A travel agency
    (C) An employment center
    (D) A driving school

93. What will take place on May 15 ?

    (A) A tour
    (B) A luncheon
    (C) An interview
    (D) A seminar

94. What can the listeners do on a Web site?

    (A) Register for an event
    (B) Read some comments
    (C) Download a map
    (D) View a price list

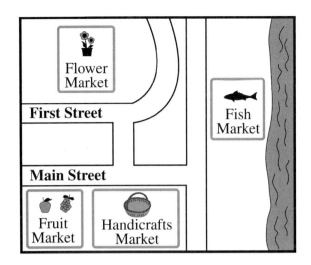

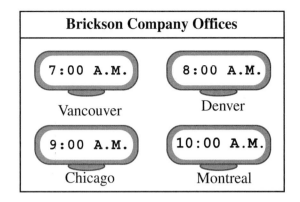

95. Look at the graphic. Which market is closed today?

(A) The flower market
(B) The fish market
(C) The handicrafts market
(D) The fruit market

96. What will the listeners do this afternoon?

(A) Meet a city official
(B) Visit a museum
(C) Attend a concert
(D) Take a boat ride

97. What does the speaker recommend that the listeners do next?

(A) Put on their name tags
(B) Take out their cameras
(C) Apply sunscreen
(D) Buy a bottle of water

98. What event is the speaker planning to attend?

(A) A retirement celebration
(B) A job interview
(C) A trade show
(D) A branch opening

99. Look at the graphic. Where is the listener's office located?

(A) In Vancouver
(B) In Denver
(C) In Chicago
(D) In Montreal

100. What does the speaker ask the listener to do?

(A) Return a phone call
(B) Provide flight information
(C) Authorize an expense
(D) Verify an address

This is the end of the Listening test.

TEST 9

토익® 정기시험
기출문제집

LC

ETS TEST

10

LISTENING TEST

In the Listening test, you will be asked to demonstrate how well you understand spoken English. The entire Listening test will last approximately 45 minutes. There are four parts, and directions are given for each part. You must mark your answers on the separate answer sheet. Do not write your answers in your test book.

PART 1

Directions: For each question in this part, you will hear four statements about a picture in your test book. When you hear the statements, you must select the one statement that best describes what you see in the picture. Then find the number of the question on your answer sheet and mark your answer. The statements will not be printed in your test book and will be spoken only one time.

Statement (C), "They're sitting at a table," is the best description of the picture, so you should select answer (C) and mark it on your answer sheet.

1.

2.

GO ON TO THE NEXT PAGE ➤

3.

4.

5.

6.

GO ON TO THE NEXT PAGE

TEST 10

PART 2

Directions: You will hear a question or statement and three responses spoken in English. They will not be printed in your test book and will be spoken only one time. Select the best response to the question or statement and mark the letter (A), (B), or (C) on your answer sheet.

7. Mark your answer on your answer sheet.

8. Mark your answer on your answer sheet.

9. Mark your answer on your answer sheet.

10. Mark your answer on your answer sheet.

11. Mark your answer on your answer sheet.

12. Mark your answer on your answer sheet.

13. Mark your answer on your answer sheet.

14. Mark your answer on your answer sheet.

15. Mark your answer on your answer sheet.

16. Mark your answer on your answer sheet.

17. Mark your answer on your answer sheet.

18. Mark your answer on your answer sheet.

19. Mark your answer on your answer sheet.

20. Mark your answer on your answer sheet.

21. Mark your answer on your answer sheet.

22. Mark your answer on your answer sheet.

23. Mark your answer on your answer sheet.

24. Mark your answer on your answer sheet.

25. Mark your answer on your answer sheet.

26. Mark your answer on your answer sheet.

27. Mark your answer on your answer sheet.

28. Mark your answer on your answer sheet.

29. Mark your answer on your answer sheet.

30. Mark your answer on your answer sheet.

31. Mark your answer on your answer sheet.

Directions: You will hear some conversations between two or more people. You will be asked to answer three questions about what the speakers say in each conversation. Select the best response to each question and mark the letter (A), (B), (C), or (D) on your answer sheet. The conversations will not be printed in your test book and will be spoken only one time.

32. Where does the woman work?

(A) At a computer store
(B) At an accounting firm
(C) At a medical clinic
(D) At a post office

33. Why is the man calling?

(A) To change an appointment
(B) To discuss a billing error
(C) To buy some supplies
(D) To ask for directions

34. According to the woman, what happened last month?

(A) Some software was installed.
(B) A business relocated.
(C) A schedule changed.
(D) Some shipments were delayed.

35. What is happening next weekend?

(A) A retirement dinner
(B) A grand opening
(C) A birthday party
(D) A wedding

36. What is the woman's specialty?

(A) Baking cakes
(B) Cooking vegetarian meals
(C) Designing kitchens
(D) Arranging flowers

37. What will the woman most likely do next?

(A) Clean a workstation
(B) Choose an assistant
(C) Look at an order form
(D) Find some equipment

38. Who is the woman?

(A) A financial adviser
(B) An art gallery owner
(C) A delivery driver
(D) An apartment manager

39. What problem does the man mention?

(A) A room is poorly lit.
(B) A machine is too noisy.
(C) A space is too small.
(D) A location is inconvenient.

40. What does the woman offer to do for the man?

(A) Renovate a room
(B) Lower a price
(C) Hire a technician
(D) Rent an appliance

41. Where do the speakers work?

(A) At a botanical garden
(B) At a landscaping company
(C) At a jewelry shop
(D) At a travel agency

42. What did the woman recently do?

(A) She made a large sale.
(B) She finalized a budget.
(C) She organized activities for a celebration.
(D) She received a certificate.

43. What will the woman do next?

(A) Give a tour
(B) Read a manual
(C) Call a vendor
(D) Rearrange a display

TEST 10

GO ON TO THE NEXT PAGE

44. Where is the man going?

(A) To a trade show
(B) To a community festival
(C) To a board meeting
(D) To an orientation session

45. What does the man mean when he says, "It's just one small bag"?

(A) He does not have space to bring an item.
(B) He does not need help.
(C) He thinks a product is too expensive.
(D) He needs to buy new luggage.

46. Why is the man leaving early?

(A) He has to catch a flight.
(B) He needs time to eat lunch.
(C) He is worried about traffic.
(D) He has to practice a presentation.

---

47. Where most likely are the speakers?

(A) At a train station
(B) At a movie theater
(C) At a restaurant
(D) At a furniture store

48. What will begin at two o'clock?

(A) A building inspection
(B) A press conference
(C) An awards ceremony
(D) A job fair

49. Why do the men decide to call a business?

(A) To order tickets
(B) To get driving directions
(C) To complain about a service
(D) To make a reservation

---

50. Where do the speakers most likely work?

(A) At a car manufacturer
(B) At a law firm
(C) At an Internet-service provider
(D) At a fashion magazine

51. What are the speakers mainly discussing?

(A) A staff assignment
(B) A salary increase
(C) A safety procedure
(D) An equipment upgrade

52. What does the man offer to do?

(A) Review a portfolio
(B) Consult a colleague
(C) Submit an application
(D) Schedule a business trip

---

53. Where do the speakers work?

(A) At an employment agency
(B) At a bank
(C) At a pharmacy
(D) At a supermarket

54. Why does the woman say, "I'll probably have to work late tonight"?

(A) To offer a solution to a problem
(B) To decline an invitation
(C) To ask for some help
(D) To correct a misunderstanding

55. What does the woman say she has to do by tomorrow?

(A) Review a résumé
(B) Set up a display
(C) Prepare a demonstration
(D) Finish a summary

---

56. Why is the woman late?

(A) She could not find a tool.
(B) She did not submit a report on time.
(C) She had to park far away.
(D) She was waiting for an assistant.

57. What problem does the man mention?

(A) Some signs are missing.
(B) Some floor tiles are loose.
(C) A handrail is broken.
(D) Some lights will not turn on.

58. What does the man say he will do after lunch?

(A) Change a light bulb
(B) Lock a room
(C) Conduct an interview
(D) Get a supervisor's approval

59. What business does the woman work for?

(A) A software company
(B) A stationery store
(C) A real estate agency
(D) An accounting firm

60. What does the woman want to do?

(A) Purchase a printer
(B) Dispose of old documents
(C) Renew a lease
(D) Ship some boxes

61. What will Raj most likely do next week?

(A) Meet the woman at her office
(B) Send the woman a catalog
(C) Attend a small-business seminar
(D) Pick up flyers from a printshop

Personal Trainer Schedule	
Monday/Tuesday	Maria
Wednesday/Thursday	Ali
Friday	Lior
Saturday/Sunday	Ema

62. What is the man's job?

(A) Flight attendant
(B) Taxi driver
(C) Hotel manager
(D) Salesperson

63. Look at the graphic. Who will the man's trainer most likely be?

(A) Maria
(B) Ali
(C) Lior
(D) Ema

64. Why does the woman make an appointment for the man?

(A) He has to take a fitness assessment.
(B) He has to complete some paperwork.
(C) He wants to practice using some equipment.
(D) He wants to tour a fitness center.

GO ON TO THE NEXT PAGE

Store Floor Plan

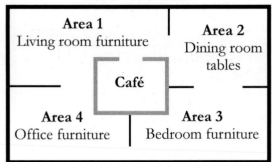

65. Why is the man at the store?

    (A) To interview for a job
    (B) To make a delivery
    (C) To complain about a service
    (D) To buy some merchandise

66. Look at the graphic. Where does the woman direct the man to go to?

    (A) Area 1
    (B) Area 2
    (C) Area 3
    (D) Area 4

67. What does the man show the woman?

    (A) An invoice
    (B) A discount coupon
    (C) A corporate policy
    (D) A product brochure

68. What does the man say he likes about his current job?

    (A) His boss is supportive.
    (B) His company offers bonuses.
    (C) The office is close to his home.
    (D) The work is interesting.

69. Look at the graphic. Which job will the man most likely apply for?

    (A) Senior Accountant
    (B) Tax Accountant
    (C) Property Accountant
    (D) Management Accountant

70. What does the woman say she will do soon?

    (A) Start her own company
    (B) Transfer to another department
    (C) Plan a vacation
    (D) Go to graduate school

PART 4

Directions: You will hear some talks given by a single speaker. You will be asked to answer three questions about what the speaker says in each talk. Select the best response to each question and mark the letter (A), (B), (C), or (D) on your answer sheet. The talks will not be printed in your test book and will be spoken only one time.

71. Where does the speaker most likely work?

(A) At a bank
(B) At an electronics store
(C) At a printshop
(D) At a museum

72. What does the speaker say he has e-mailed?

(A) An invoice
(B) A brochure
(C) A trade-show calendar
(D) A reference letter

73. What does the speaker ask the listener to do on a Web site?

(A) Sign a document
(B) Fill out a survey
(C) Submit an application
(D) Register for a class

74. Who is the intended audience for the announcement?

(A) Cooks
(B) Customers
(C) Waiters
(D) Hosts

75. Which menu item does the speaker mention?

(A) A soup
(B) A salad
(C) A main course
(D) A dessert

76. What does the speaker ask Mark to do?

(A) Sort through some food items
(B) Apologize to a customer
(C) Stay for a later shift
(D) Clean some dishes

77. What is the focus of the workshop?

(A) Interviewing techniques
(B) Leadership skills
(C) Collecting consumer feedback
(D) Time-management tips

78. What should the listeners do at home?

(A) Create a schedule
(B) Work on a résumé
(C) Read some articles
(D) Watch a video

79. Why does the speaker say, "Kenta has worked here for over twenty years"?

(A) To announce Kenta's retirement
(B) To explain Kenta's promotion
(C) To recommend Kenta's services
(D) To agree with Kenta's opinion

80. What type of event is taking place this evening?

(A) A holiday parade
(B) An arts fair
(C) A music concert
(D) A sports competition

81. What does the speaker advise the listeners to do?

(A) Save their tickets
(B) Take public transportation
(C) Bring a camera
(D) Arrive early

82. What will the listeners hear next?

(A) A celebrity speech
(B) A weather report
(C) A new song
(D) A business update

GO ON TO THE NEXT PAGE

83. What does the listener want help with?

(A) Completing a building design
(B) Planning a grand opening
(C) Selling a home
(D) Purchasing furniture

84. What does the speaker say she will do first?

(A) Get city approval
(B) Contact a bank
(C) Submit a payment
(D) Visit a property

85. Why is the speaker unable to meet until next week?

(A) She will be out of town.
(B) She is busy with another client.
(C) Her car is being repaired.
(D) Her house is being renovated.

86. Who most likely is the speaker?

(A) A health inspector
(B) A store supervisor
(C) A maintenance worker
(D) An interior decorator

87. What does the speaker ask the listeners to do?

(A) Send accurate time sheets
(B) Save important documents
(C) Recommend a job candidate
(D) Keep an area neat

88. What does the speaker imply when he says, "the store's opening in a few minutes"?

(A) Customers should be patient.
(B) Employees should work quickly.
(C) A schedule was changed.
(D) A meeting is ending.

89. Who is Martina Santos?

(A) A reporter
(B) An architect
(C) An artist
(D) A gardener

90. According to the speaker, what is Martina Santos' source of inspiration?

(A) Travel
(B) Nature
(C) History
(D) Music

91. What does the speaker say the listeners can receive at the front desk?

(A) Some tickets
(B) Some headphones
(C) A receipt
(D) A postcard

92. What event is taking place?

(A) A product launch
(B) A going-away party
(C) An awards ceremony
(D) An anniversary celebration

93. Why does the speaker say, "sales of our new cosmetics line increased by ten percent"?

(A) To request additional staff
(B) To express disappointment
(C) To recognize an accomplishment
(D) To describe a new advertising strategy

94. According to the speaker, what is Alina going to do?

(A) Transfer to another location
(B) Buy a house
(C) Start a new business
(D) Write a book

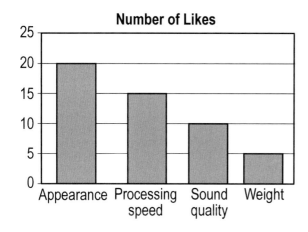

Number of Likes

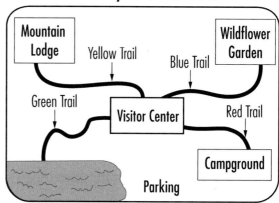

Bankbury Nature Preserve

95. According to the speaker, where did the feedback come from?

(A) A trade magazine review
(B) A board member
(C) A group of employees
(D) A marketing research firm

96. Look at the graphic. Which feature will the listeners work on?

(A) Appearance
(B) Processing speed
(C) Sound quality
(D) Weight

97. What does the speaker ask the listeners to do by the end of the week?

(A) Talk to their managers
(B) Suggest some ideas
(C) Revise some documentation
(D) Approve some specifications

98. Look at the graphic. Which trail does the speaker recommend?

(A) Yellow
(B) Blue
(C) Red
(D) Green

99. According to the speaker, what will happen at 3:00 P.M.?

(A) The bus will leave the parking area.
(B) Some team events will begin.
(C) A photograph will be taken.
(D) A park ranger will give a lecture.

100. What does the speaker say he will do next?

(A) Lead a hike
(B) Meet with the company director
(C) Distribute some beverages
(D) Go to the visitor center

This is the end of the Listening test.

TEST 10

ANSWER SHEET

토익® 정기시험 기출문제집

수험번호

응시일자 : 20   년   월   일

성명 한글
한자
영자

Test 01 (Part 1~4)

Test 02 (Part 1~4)

ANSWER SHEET

토익® 정기시험 기출문제집

한글		
한자		
영자		
성명		

수험번호

응시일자 : 20   년   월   일

Test 04 (Part 1~4)

Test 03 (Part 1~4)

ANSWER SHEET

토익® 정기시험 기출문제집

수험번호

응시일자 : 20   년   월   일

성명

| 한글 |
| 한자 |
| 영자 |

Test 05 (Part 1~4)

1				21				41
2				22				42
3				23				43
4				24				44
5				25				45
6				26				46
7				27				47
8				28				48
9				29				49
10				30				50
11				31				51
12				32				52
13				33				53
14				34				54
15				35				55
16				36				56
17				37				57
18				38				58
19				39				59
20				40				60

Test 06 (Part 1~4)

1				21				41
2				22				42
3				23				43
4				24				44
5				25				45
6				26				46
7				27				47
8				28				48
9				29				49
10				30				50
11				31				51
12				32				52
13				33				53
14				34				54
15				35				55
16				36				56
17				37				57
18				38				58
19				39				59
20				40				60

ANSWER SHEET

토익® 정기시험 기출문제집

수험번호 | | | | | | |

응시일자 : 20 년 월 일

성명	
한 글	
한 자	
영 자	

Test 07 (Part 1~4)

1	ⓐ ⓑ ⓒ ⓓ	21	ⓐ ⓑ ⓒ	41	ⓐ ⓑ ⓒ ⓓ	61	ⓐ ⓑ ⓒ ⓓ	81	ⓐ ⓑ ⓒ ⓓ
2	ⓐ ⓑ ⓒ ⓓ	22	ⓐ ⓑ ⓒ	42	ⓐ ⓑ ⓒ ⓓ	62	ⓐ ⓑ ⓒ ⓓ	82	ⓐ ⓑ ⓒ ⓓ
3	ⓐ ⓑ ⓒ ⓓ	23	ⓐ ⓑ ⓒ	43	ⓐ ⓑ ⓒ ⓓ	63	ⓐ ⓑ ⓒ ⓓ	83	ⓐ ⓑ ⓒ ⓓ
4	ⓐ ⓑ ⓒ ⓓ	24	ⓐ ⓑ ⓒ	44	ⓐ ⓑ ⓒ ⓓ	64	ⓐ ⓑ ⓒ ⓓ	84	ⓐ ⓑ ⓒ ⓓ
5	ⓐ ⓑ ⓒ ⓓ	25	ⓐ ⓑ ⓒ	45	ⓐ ⓑ ⓒ ⓓ	65	ⓐ ⓑ ⓒ ⓓ	85	ⓐ ⓑ ⓒ ⓓ
6	ⓐ ⓑ ⓒ ⓓ	26	ⓐ ⓑ ⓒ	46	ⓐ ⓑ ⓒ ⓓ	66	ⓐ ⓑ ⓒ ⓓ	86	ⓐ ⓑ ⓒ ⓓ
7	ⓐ ⓑ ⓒ	27	ⓐ ⓑ ⓒ	47	ⓐ ⓑ ⓒ ⓓ	67	ⓐ ⓑ ⓒ ⓓ	87	ⓐ ⓑ ⓒ ⓓ
8	ⓐ ⓑ ⓒ	28	ⓐ ⓑ ⓒ	48	ⓐ ⓑ ⓒ ⓓ	68	ⓐ ⓑ ⓒ ⓓ	88	ⓐ ⓑ ⓒ ⓓ
9	ⓐ ⓑ ⓒ	29	ⓐ ⓑ ⓒ	49	ⓐ ⓑ ⓒ ⓓ	69	ⓐ ⓑ ⓒ ⓓ	89	ⓐ ⓑ ⓒ ⓓ
10	ⓐ ⓑ ⓒ	30	ⓐ ⓑ ⓒ	50	ⓐ ⓑ ⓒ ⓓ	70	ⓐ ⓑ ⓒ ⓓ	90	ⓐ ⓑ ⓒ ⓓ
11	ⓐ ⓑ ⓒ	31	ⓐ ⓑ ⓒ	51	ⓐ ⓑ ⓒ ⓓ	71	ⓐ ⓑ ⓒ ⓓ	91	ⓐ ⓑ ⓒ ⓓ
12	ⓐ ⓑ ⓒ	32	ⓐ ⓑ ⓒ ⓓ	52	ⓐ ⓑ ⓒ ⓓ	72	ⓐ ⓑ ⓒ ⓓ	92	ⓐ ⓑ ⓒ ⓓ
13	ⓐ ⓑ ⓒ	33	ⓐ ⓑ ⓒ ⓓ	53	ⓐ ⓑ ⓒ ⓓ	73	ⓐ ⓑ ⓒ ⓓ	93	ⓐ ⓑ ⓒ ⓓ
14	ⓐ ⓑ ⓒ	34	ⓐ ⓑ ⓒ ⓓ	54	ⓐ ⓑ ⓒ ⓓ	74	ⓐ ⓑ ⓒ ⓓ	94	ⓐ ⓑ ⓒ ⓓ
15	ⓐ ⓑ ⓒ	35	ⓐ ⓑ ⓒ ⓓ	55	ⓐ ⓑ ⓒ ⓓ	75	ⓐ ⓑ ⓒ ⓓ	95	ⓐ ⓑ ⓒ ⓓ
16	ⓐ ⓑ ⓒ	36	ⓐ ⓑ ⓒ ⓓ	56	ⓐ ⓑ ⓒ ⓓ	76	ⓐ ⓑ ⓒ ⓓ	96	ⓐ ⓑ ⓒ ⓓ
17	ⓐ ⓑ ⓒ	37	ⓐ ⓑ ⓒ ⓓ	57	ⓐ ⓑ ⓒ ⓓ	77	ⓐ ⓑ ⓒ ⓓ	97	ⓐ ⓑ ⓒ ⓓ
18	ⓐ ⓑ ⓒ	38	ⓐ ⓑ ⓒ ⓓ	58	ⓐ ⓑ ⓒ ⓓ	78	ⓐ ⓑ ⓒ ⓓ	98	ⓐ ⓑ ⓒ ⓓ
19	ⓐ ⓑ ⓒ	39	ⓐ ⓑ ⓒ ⓓ	59	ⓐ ⓑ ⓒ ⓓ	79	ⓐ ⓑ ⓒ ⓓ	99	ⓐ ⓑ ⓒ ⓓ
20	ⓐ ⓑ ⓒ	40	ⓐ ⓑ ⓒ ⓓ	60	ⓐ ⓑ ⓒ ⓓ	80	ⓐ ⓑ ⓒ ⓓ	100	ⓐ ⓑ ⓒ ⓓ

Test 08 (Part 1~4)

1	ⓐ ⓑ ⓒ ⓓ	21	ⓐ ⓑ ⓒ	41	ⓐ ⓑ ⓒ ⓓ	61	ⓐ ⓑ ⓒ ⓓ	81	ⓐ ⓑ ⓒ ⓓ
2	ⓐ ⓑ ⓒ ⓓ	22	ⓐ ⓑ ⓒ	42	ⓐ ⓑ ⓒ ⓓ	62	ⓐ ⓑ ⓒ ⓓ	82	ⓐ ⓑ ⓒ ⓓ
3	ⓐ ⓑ ⓒ ⓓ	23	ⓐ ⓑ ⓒ	43	ⓐ ⓑ ⓒ ⓓ	63	ⓐ ⓑ ⓒ ⓓ	83	ⓐ ⓑ ⓒ ⓓ
4	ⓐ ⓑ ⓒ ⓓ	24	ⓐ ⓑ ⓒ	44	ⓐ ⓑ ⓒ ⓓ	64	ⓐ ⓑ ⓒ ⓓ	84	ⓐ ⓑ ⓒ ⓓ
5	ⓐ ⓑ ⓒ ⓓ	25	ⓐ ⓑ ⓒ	45	ⓐ ⓑ ⓒ ⓓ	65	ⓐ ⓑ ⓒ ⓓ	85	ⓐ ⓑ ⓒ ⓓ
6	ⓐ ⓑ ⓒ ⓓ	26	ⓐ ⓑ ⓒ	46	ⓐ ⓑ ⓒ ⓓ	66	ⓐ ⓑ ⓒ ⓓ	86	ⓐ ⓑ ⓒ ⓓ
7	ⓐ ⓑ ⓒ	27	ⓐ ⓑ ⓒ	47	ⓐ ⓑ ⓒ ⓓ	67	ⓐ ⓑ ⓒ ⓓ	87	ⓐ ⓑ ⓒ ⓓ
8	ⓐ ⓑ ⓒ	28	ⓐ ⓑ ⓒ	48	ⓐ ⓑ ⓒ ⓓ	68	ⓐ ⓑ ⓒ ⓓ	88	ⓐ ⓑ ⓒ ⓓ
9	ⓐ ⓑ ⓒ	29	ⓐ ⓑ ⓒ	49	ⓐ ⓑ ⓒ ⓓ	69	ⓐ ⓑ ⓒ ⓓ	89	ⓐ ⓑ ⓒ ⓓ
10	ⓐ ⓑ ⓒ	30	ⓐ ⓑ ⓒ	50	ⓐ ⓑ ⓒ ⓓ	70	ⓐ ⓑ ⓒ ⓓ	90	ⓐ ⓑ ⓒ ⓓ
11	ⓐ ⓑ ⓒ	31	ⓐ ⓑ ⓒ	51	ⓐ ⓑ ⓒ ⓓ	71	ⓐ ⓑ ⓒ ⓓ	91	ⓐ ⓑ ⓒ ⓓ
12	ⓐ ⓑ ⓒ	32	ⓐ ⓑ ⓒ ⓓ	52	ⓐ ⓑ ⓒ ⓓ	72	ⓐ ⓑ ⓒ ⓓ	92	ⓐ ⓑ ⓒ ⓓ
13	ⓐ ⓑ ⓒ	33	ⓐ ⓑ ⓒ ⓓ	53	ⓐ ⓑ ⓒ ⓓ	73	ⓐ ⓑ ⓒ ⓓ	93	ⓐ ⓑ ⓒ ⓓ
14	ⓐ ⓑ ⓒ	34	ⓐ ⓑ ⓒ ⓓ	54	ⓐ ⓑ ⓒ ⓓ	74	ⓐ ⓑ ⓒ ⓓ	94	ⓐ ⓑ ⓒ ⓓ
15	ⓐ ⓑ ⓒ	35	ⓐ ⓑ ⓒ ⓓ	55	ⓐ ⓑ ⓒ ⓓ	75	ⓐ ⓑ ⓒ ⓓ	95	ⓐ ⓑ ⓒ ⓓ
16	ⓐ ⓑ ⓒ	36	ⓐ ⓑ ⓒ ⓓ	56	ⓐ ⓑ ⓒ ⓓ	76	ⓐ ⓑ ⓒ ⓓ	96	ⓐ ⓑ ⓒ ⓓ
17	ⓐ ⓑ ⓒ	37	ⓐ ⓑ ⓒ ⓓ	57	ⓐ ⓑ ⓒ ⓓ	77	ⓐ ⓑ ⓒ ⓓ	97	ⓐ ⓑ ⓒ ⓓ
18	ⓐ ⓑ ⓒ	38	ⓐ ⓑ ⓒ ⓓ	58	ⓐ ⓑ ⓒ ⓓ	78	ⓐ ⓑ ⓒ ⓓ	98	ⓐ ⓑ ⓒ ⓓ
19	ⓐ ⓑ ⓒ	39	ⓐ ⓑ ⓒ ⓓ	59	ⓐ ⓑ ⓒ ⓓ	79	ⓐ ⓑ ⓒ ⓓ	99	ⓐ ⓑ ⓒ ⓓ
20	ⓐ ⓑ ⓒ	40	ⓐ ⓑ ⓒ ⓓ	60	ⓐ ⓑ ⓒ ⓓ	80	ⓐ ⓑ ⓒ ⓓ	100	ⓐ ⓑ ⓒ ⓓ

ANSWER SHEET

토익® 정기시험 기출문제집

수험번호

응시일자 : 20 년 월 일

성명: 한글 / 한자 / 영자

Test 09 (Part 1~4)

1	2	3	...	20	21	...	40	41	...	60	61	...	80	81	...	100

Test 10 (Part 1~4)

1	2	3	...	20	21	...	40	41	...	60	61	...	80	81	...	100